KV-582-414

Creative Learning in Perspective

Creative Learning in Perspective

Tudor Powell Jones

UNIVERSITY OF LONDON PRESS LTD

/55·3
JON

ISBN 0 340 14900 0 Boards ✓   010 8914
ISBN 0 340 14901 9 Unibook

University of London Press Ltd
St Paul's House, Warwick Lane, London EC4P 4AH

Printed in Great Britain by
Butler & Tanner Ltd, Frome and London

Contents

Preface

In the past the term 'creativity' has carried with it an aura of exclusiveness. Creative people were thought to be geniuses, who possessed some rare, innate qualities that raised them above the non-creative mass of humanity. In recent years, however, the term has lost its earlier connotation, and is now often used in the sense of 'originality', 'progressiveness', 'novelty', or indeed to describe anything that deviates from the norm.

Scientific research, especially in the last decade, has led to a deeper understanding and a more realistic approach to creativity, giving educationists the knowledge that all are born with creative potential; and, given proper environment and techniques, this potential can be recognised, nurtured and measured.

Most people, however, still have no clear idea of what creativity really means because the task of encouraging it is comparatively new.

All who are concerned with the development of children—parents, teachers, and the intelligent public—need to understand the nature of the creative urge to enable it to develop and express itself. This book was prepared in order to satisfy this need.

While the emphasis in every chapter is on clarifying the term creativity and on placing it in perspective, the more experienced educationists will be helped in their studies and guided in extending their information in two ways—first, by the numerous references and secondly, by the problems discussed: problems that lead to questions most frequently asked by teachers and parents. *Chapter one* analyses the many concepts of creativity and its relationship to intelligence, and attempts to find a working definition.

Chapter two examines the characteristics of creative learning, the levels and stages in its psychological development.

Chapter three outlines the difficulties which confront the creative worker, and describes the school atmosphere and educational principles which make creative learning possible.

Chapter four shows the limitations of an exclusively creative approach to learning, and in a number of sections suggests activities which should operate in each curricular area. Consideration is given to school organisation and teacher training.

Chapter five examines the methods of measuring creativity and questions the desirability of such measurement.

Chapter six considers the implications of a more creative education in the British society of the future.

CHAPTER ONE

What is Creativity?

When Russia succeeded in getting into space first with Sputnik 1, the Western world, and the United States in particular, was shaken into studying the type of learning which was producing Russian scientists. In the West, industry had been clamouring for more creative scientists and engineers and the Cold War demanded ingenious defence devices. Conventional learning in schools and a conformist attitude were said to contribute to this failure to compete in the space-race. It was realised that, because of their education and training, the vast majority of Western scientists were convergent in their thinking. They excelled in close reasoning and intelligence tests which called for conventional responses, but lacked the power of imagination and were loath to leave the beaten track of accepted ideas. What was urgently needed was more divergent thinking, which excels in original, imaginative and unusual ideas rather than in deductive logic. The productive physical scientist became the cult figure of the creativity movement in the U.S.A.

This concern for producing creative scientists had far-reaching repercussions which affected every branch of learning. Society recognised an over-intellectualism and a lack of spontaneity in its thinking which made it thoroughly unproductive, and so exaggerated concern for creativity developed in the younger generation. It appeared that American educationists in particular went out of their way to sell 'creativity'. Creative learning became a most flourishing educational fad, an obsession, and a panacea. Dr Liam Hudson, now Professor of Educational Sciences in the University of Edinburgh, was particularly watchful and critical of the movement. 'Creativity is a bandwagon,' he wrote, 'a boom in the American psychological industry.'

Creativity is, of course, far more than this, and the movement towards creativeness has, whatever its short-comings, inspired improved learning in many British schools. Where before there was convergence, reproduction and manipulation, now there is to be found education concerned with discovery, divergence and imagination.

Before examining the full implications of this movement in the schools, it is necessary to consider the relationship between creativity and intelligence. American educational psychologists have tended to maintain that the two are distinct abilities. British educational psychologists, particularly Burt and Vernon, have held that without a high degree of intelligence no one is likely to produce creative results that are worth while. What seems clear is that creativity does not depend on intelligence alone.

In the past the term 'gifted child' became synonymous with 'child with a high I.Q.', concealing other accomplishments. But intelligence tests measure the capacity to recall, recognise, and solve rather than to invent or innovate. Yet learning involves innovation as well as remembering, discovery as well as recollection, and it has been felt that these tests did not represent an adequate range of all mental abilities. The publication of the new British Intelligence Scale, produced by the British Psychological Society, has been held back by the untimely death (1969) of Professor F. W. Warburton. This scale contains a 'creativity' section, and its appearance is eagerly awaited.

Getzels and Jackson (1962) made the first major attempt to demonstrate a cognitive dimension in children which could be described as creativity and to distinguish it from general intelligence. They did not question the value of the I.Q. as a measurement but pointed out its limitations. They held that although I.Q. was the best single predictive measure of subsequent academic success or failure, many other variables affected school achievement. Some of these are the qualities summarised by the term 'creativity'. A detailed study was made between two groups of middle-class adolescent pupils in a school in the Middle West, near Chicago. One group was relatively high in intelligence and low in creativity, the other high in creativity but relatively low in intelligence. Interesting differences were found between the 'highly creative' and the 'highly intelligent' groups. The highly creative group, in spite of a mean I.Q. lower by 23 points, was superior in scholastic achievements when tested. But despite this apparent over-achievement, the 'creatives' were less popular with their teachers because they were less conforming and were less anxious for success.

The main conclusion reached by Getzels and Jackson was that at a fairly high level of intelligence (120 to 130 and above), intelligence and creativity were sufficiently independent to discriminate between the two. Many critics maintained that this claim was not justified because of inadequate procedures by which the data were obtained and interpretation of the data. The number of children used was limited and not typical, and many of the instruments used were specific and unstandardised. However, the authors were fully aware of the limitations of their inquiry, and their work must be regarded as an important exploratory study on which further research could be based.

Several subsequent researchers have suggested that the correlation between measures of creativity and intelligence is much higher than Getzels and Jackson found in their rather special sample, but both Torrance (1962) and Mackinnon (1962) agreed that above an I.Q. of around 120, a higher intelligence caused little difference in creative ability and that it was creativity that determined success. Torrance described as a familiar figure the high I.Q. individual who does well in academic tasks but is incapable of original thought. Receptivity does not always mean creativity, and Mackinnon discovered that the highly creative men and women he studied could not be distinguished from their contemporaries by their score in intelligence tests.

Liam Hudson (1966), in a very interesting book, *Contrary Imaginations*, described experiments with English public and grammar schoolboys, and shared the view expressed by Getzels and Jackson that the more intelligent person is not necessarily the more creative one. He made certain observations which had not emerged from American research. He questioned the assumption that people who score well on tests of divergent thinking are thereby shown to be more creative. He considered that both convergent and divergent thinking could result in a creative product. He also found a close relationship between divergent thinkers and arts specialists and between convergent thinkers and scientists.

The parallel between divergent thinking and creativity has been too lightly assumed, but Hudson concludes over-readily that convergent and divergent thinkers are distinct types which do not overlap. The great majority of people are both divergent and convergent thinkers according to situation, type of problem and motivation.

The most detailed and methodologically satisfying attempt to obtain a reliable overall assessment of children's creativity and the extent to which it is distinguishable from intelligence came from Wallach and Kogan (1965). They adopted the Getzels and Jackson method of forming contrasting groups of children (10- to 11-year-olds) high in creative ability and low in intelligence and vice-versa. They divided their large sample into four groups. The 'High Creativity–High Intelligence' children could exercise both control and freedom. The 'High Creativity–Low Intelligence' children were in angry conflict with themselves and beset by feelings of inadequacy. Yet in a stress-free environment they could fulfil themselves with understanding. The 'Low Creativity–High Intelligence' group were found to be addicted to school achievement which was their main goal and interest in life. The 'Low Creativity–Low Intelligence' group were apprehensive. Wallach and Kogan concluded, not unreasonably, that a dimension of intellectual ability existed which was independent of general intellectual ability, and was appropriately called 'creativity'—a mode of perception-functioning which matters a great deal in the life of every individual.

Conflicting evidence came from Lovell and Shields (1967) who compared scores gained by the children on creativity tests not only with the scores gained on I.Q. tests, but also with the scores gained on the tests of logical thinking and the tests of mathematical ability. They reported the existence of a strong component of intelligence common to all the tasks which the children completed, and suggested that creativity tests[1] do not measure intellectual abilities entirely independent of those measured by conventional I.Q. tests.

Dacey, Madaus and Allen (1969) studied and tested a number of Irish public grammar schoolboys. In this sample, divergent thinking and intelligence emerged as separate phenomena. There was also a separation between the verbal and non-verbal thinking measures, but this was not as clear as between divergent thinking and intelligence. These results were very similar to those found by Madaus (1967) working alone with an American sample.

These various findings suggest a definite relationship between

---

[1]   The measurement of creativity is examined in detail in Chapter Five.

intelligence quotient and creativity measures. Intelligence and creativity are by no means synonymous, but one cannot exist without the other. The presence of one, however, is no guarantee of the presence of the other to the same degree. It is generally accepted that creative thinking abilities do exist, and that they can be measured.

The nature of these creative thinking abilities must now be examined and a working definition devised on which to base learning activities.

The word 'creativity' does not appear in better-known dictionaries, and it would seem that the word describes not *one* individual ability but a sum total of different factors. These factors can be defined in terms of the product and in terms of the process itself. The numerous definitions available have concentrated on four factors—relationship of elements, conflict, problem-solving, and the environment.

Getzels and Jackson (1962) defined creativity as 'conjoining elements that are customarily thought of as independent and dissimilar'. This view of the creative act as relating separate ideas or processes was supported by S. A. and M. T. Mednick (1964)—creative thinking, in their view consists of 'forming new combinations of associative elements which either meet specified requirements, or are in some way useful'. Koestler (1964) argued that it was only when Archimedes perceived the link between the weight–volume matrix and the displacement matrix that he was able to reach a creative solution. It was the linkage between two separate entities that formed the basis of his creative thinking. These views, then, claim that creativeness is simply a process of arranging well-known facts into new relationships so that results may be achieved more effectively. The connection nearly always occurs as a flash of insight and is the result of subconscious thought processes.

Freud and his followers stressed the important part which mental conflict plays in the birth of creativeness, and claimed that it was the creative person who solved his conflicts rewardingly. Deutsch (1960), a neo-Freudian, believed that creativity was an unconscious defence against mental illness. He held that fantasies which occur in the preliminary stage of mental illness were similar to the fantasies of the creative person, but that the neurotic merely imagines that desirable changes have occurred, whereas the creative worker brings about those desired changes. Barron

(1958) claimed that healthy persons with well-adjusted personalities need a temporary upset as a pre-requisite for creative
experience. J. S. Bruner (1962) talked of the importance of
'effective surprise' and a 'shock of recognition' as an effect art
often had on the observer, and Liam Hudson (1966) affirms this
general view that creativity, 'if not born of unhappiness is born
certainly of unease'.

Einstein and Infeld had asserted that the formulation of a
problem is more important than the solution to it, and there have
been a number of definitions of creativity as a specific form of
problem-solving behaviour characterised by originality (that is,
the production of a new solution). The first stage must be the
recognition of a problem. Margaret Wason (1968) defined
creativity as 'a way of operating cognitively, aesthetically and
emotionally which will find problems in a situation or material
and will try and solve them'. Getzels and Csikzentmihalyi (1967)
defined creative thinking as 'the posing of a problem as well as
the action of trying to solve it'. The creative aspect of problem-
solving is characterised by personal expression and personal discovery, and Torrance's (1962) definition of creative thinking was
'the process of sensing gaps or missing elements and forming ideas
or hypotheses concerning them'. The degree of creativity according to this view depends on a person's realtive sensitivity to problems and his ability to think of or visualise a problem situation.

There is a number of educationists who support the view that
environmental factors are of supreme importance to creativity.
Just as later personal relationships reflect earler relationships with
parents, so adult interests echo earlier interests. A definite continuity of development exists between the child's experiences and
fantasies and the controlled imagination of the creative adult.
Weinsberg and Springer (1967) explain creativity in terms of
environment. They claim that the product of a home which
fosters 'expressiveness without domination' and the absence of
complete dependence of children on parents strengthens individuality. Getzels and Jackson (1962) found evidence of a more
permissive parental upbringing among creative children. Similarly Liam Hudson (1966) theorises that the differences between
convergent and divergent thinkers are developed from early
experience in the environment. There is no general agreement as
to what constitutes a good home for the development of creative
thinkers.

The complexity of creativity makes it almost impossible to have a universally-acceptable definition, so that the factors we have considered, and many others, must be regarded as descriptive rather than explanatory. Creativeness is not a single factor, but rather a collection of different abilities, every single one of which can be possessed in different degrees by every individual. Persons who are evidently creative will be endowed with creative abilities which may be thought of as generalised intellectual skills which can be developed through appropriate practice.

The process of creativity is so complex that to define it too precisely might do it a disservice. But after considering the various factors closely connected with the process—relationship of elements, conflict, problem-solving, and the environment—it is possible to arrive at a flexible working definition on which to base future discussion on creativity and on which to build a plan of creative work for schools:

> *Creativity is a combination of flexibility, originality and sensitivity to ideas which enables the thinker to break away from usual sequences of thought into different and productive sequences, the result of which gives satisfaction to himself and possibly to others.*

As a result of this process, a novel product emerges which has grown out of the uniqueness of an individual in his environment. As creativity is the result both of the systematic and the artistic, it is possible in both the arts and the sciences. The product of creative thought may be new for society, or merely new to the individual who produces it, but what is essential is that it should bring joy to its creator.

References

BARRON, F. 'The Psychology of Imagination'. *Scientific American*, **199**, 50, 1958 (151).

BRUNER, J. S. *On Knowing: Essays for the Left Hand*. Cambridge, Mass.: Harvard University Press, 1962.

DACEY, J., MADAUS, G. F., and ALLEN, A. 'The Relationship of Creativity and Intelligence in Irish Adolescents'. *British Journal of Educational Psychology*, **39**, 3, 1969.

DEUTSCH, M. *Minority Group and Class Status as related to Social and Personality Factors in Scholastic Achievement. Monograph*

No. 2. Ithaca, New York: Society for Applied Anthropology, 1960.

EINSTEIN, A., and INFIELD, L. *Evolution of Physics.* London: Cambridge University Press, 1938.

GETZELS, J. W., and CSIKZENTMIHALYI, M. 'Creative Thinking'. *Science Journal,* September 1967.

GETZELS, J. W., and JACKSON, P. W. *Creativity and Intelligence: Explorations with Gifted Students.* New York: John Wiley, 1962.

HUDSON, L. *Contrary Imaginations.* London: Methuen, 1966.

LOVELL, K., and SHIELDS, J. B. 'Some Aspects of the Gifted Child'. *British Journal of Educational Psychology,* 37

MACKINNON, D. W. 'The Nature and Nurture of Creative Talent'. *American Psychologist,* **17,** 1962.

MADAUS, G. F. 'Divergent Thinking and Intelligence'. *Journal of Educational Measurement,* **4,** 1967 (227–35).

TORRANCE, E. P. *Guiding Creative Talent.* Englewood Cliffs, N.J.: Prentice-Hall, 1962.

WALLACH, M., and KOGAN, N. *Modes of thinking in Young Children.* New York: Holt, Rinehart and Winston, 1965.

WARBURTON, F. W. 'Construction of the New British Intelligence Scale: Progress report'. *Bulletin of the British Psychological Society,* 1966.

WASON, M. O. 'Creativity in Schools'. *New Era,* **49,** February 1968.

WEINSBERG, P. S., and SPRINGER, K. J. 'Environmental Factors in Creative Function'. In MOONEY, K., and ROGIK, T. (eds.) *Explorations in Creativity.* New York: Harper, 1967.

Further Reading

ADRIAN, E. D. *The Physical Background of Perception.* Oxford: Oxford University Press, 1947.

ANDERSON, H. H. (ed.) *Creativity and its Cultivation.* New York: Harper, 1959.

BARRON, F. 'The Disposition towards Originality'. *Journal of Abnormal and Social Psychology,* **51,** 1955 (478–85).

BRAIN, W. R. *Diseases of the Nervous System.* Oxford: Oxford University Press, 1947.

BRUNER, J. S. *The Process of Education.* Cambridge, Mass.: Harvard University Press, 1960.

BURT, C. 'Critical notice of *Creativity and Intelligence* by Getzels, J. W., and Jackson, P. W.' *British Journal of Educational Psychology*, **32**, 1962 (292–8).

CARLSON, R. K. 'Emergence of Creative Personality'. *Child Education*, **36**, 9, 1960.

CHISELIN, B. *The Creative Process*. Berkeley, Calif.: University of California Press, 1952.

CHISELIN, B. (ed.) *The Creative Process: A Symposium*. New York: New American Library, 1955.

CROPLEY, A. J. 'Creativity and Intelligence'. *British Journal of Educational Studies*, **36**, 1966.

DAVITZ, J. R. *The Communication of Emotional Meaning*. New York: McGraw-Hill, 1964.

EDWARDS, M. P., and TYLER, L. E. 'Intelligence, Creativity and Achievement in Non-selective Public Junior High School'. *Journal of Educational Psychology*, **56**, 1965.

FLESCHER, I. 'Anxiety and Achievement of Intellectually Gifted and Creatively Gifted Children'. *Journal of Psychology*, **56**, 1963.

FROMM, E. 'The Creative Attitude'. In ANDERSON, H. H. (ed.) *Creativity and its Cultivation*. New York: Harper, 1959.

GUILFORD, J. P. 'Creativity'. *American Psychologist*, **5**, 1950.

GUILFORD, J. P. 'The Structure of the Intellect'. *Psychological Bulletin*, **53**, 1956.

GUILFORD, J. P. *The Nature of Human Intelligence*. New York: McGraw-Hill, 1967.

HUDSON, L. *Frames of Mind*. London: Methuen, 1968.

HUMPHREYS, L. G. 'The Organisation of Human Ability'. *American Psychologist*, **17**, 1962.

JONES, E. *The Life and Works of Sigmund Freud* (Trilling, L., and Marcus, S. (eds.); one volume). Harmondsworth: Penguin, 1967.

KOESTLER, A. *The Act of Creation*. London: Hutchinson, 1964; reprinted Pan Books, 1966.

MEDNICK, S. A., and MEDNICK, M. T. 'An Associative Interpretation of the Creative Process'. In TAYLOR, C. W. (ed.) *Widening Horizons in Creativity*. New York: John Wiley, 1964 (54–68).

SOCIETY FOR RESEARCH INTO HIGHER EDUCATION. *Creativity: A selective review of research*. 1968.

SULTAN, E. E. 'A Factorial Study in the Domain of Creative

Thinking'. *British Journal of Educational Psychology*, **32,** 1962 (78–82).

TERMAN, L., and ODEN, M. *The Gifted Child.* Lexington, Mass.: Heath, 1951.

VERNON, P. E. 'Creativity and Intelligence'. *Educational Research*, **9,** 1964.

CHAPTER TWO

Origins and Scope of the Creative Process

A person's effort is most effective when it is sustained by some urge within himself—by curiosity, interest, or the urge to express, make, or do. The art of creation is governed by conscious thought and by emotion, both components working within a subtle and complex relationship. Our efforts to stimulate creativity will find much support in the child's inner nature and in his instinctive tendencies.

Curiosity is probably the most important factor in creativity, for its essence is to see whether new methods of expression in creative activities will prove aesthetically more satisfying. The tendency is not wholly concerned with novelty, however; it involves something which is partly familiar and partly unfamiliar. The wholly unfamiliar will pass by most individuals entirely or will arouse fear. The need for partial familiarity is essential in the creative process.

The ability to construct is evident in the human being during the first year, when the first experimental activities of handling and building with materials are followed by purposeful manipulation, selecting, assembling, and shaping. From his second year, the child will not be content merely with piling bricks and blocks on top of one another. He will proceed to make things—walls, houses, bridges, trains. The highest form of construction will merge into creativity where there is less manipulation and reproduction and more scope for the imagination and originality. In the working out of this innate tendency both familiar and unfamiliar experiences are again necessary. The early stages of the process involve both direct and indirect imitation. But imitation is not incompatible with originality. We begin in imitation, then diverge into creative originality.

Constructive ideas give a person a sense of mastery, a sense of power. The highest forms of self-assertion are also found in creative work. We have to express ourselves in order to assert our personalities and to come to terms with ourselves. Individuals must be given the opportunity to express themselves naturally, or the result will be a limitation of their creative ability. When, for example, a parent insists on doing something for a child that the child can do for himself, he suggests something negative and in-efficient about the child. If this process continues, the child will grow into adolescence and adulthood with the emotional appara-tus of a child and with a self-image that is destructive to his natural creative processes.

At both child and adult levels, creativity is experienced in play —a joyful, spontaneous activity which is an important safety-valve for repressed tendencies. In play children provide interim explanations of phenomena which would otherwise baffle them. Creative expression needs a period of play to link fantasy and reality, a period appropriately called 'Reality-Testing' by psycho-logists. Play comes first, and logical construction later, as Jean Piaget's research on stages of thinking has made clear. This need for play and fantasy in the creative process outlines what appears to be an important paradox. Despite the need for conscious effort and rationality in problem-solving, mature and creative thinking needs, at least in some degree, a period of playfulness, the fantasy of the primary thought-processes, and child-like modes of thought.

It is in the child's natural endowment, his instincts and his emotions, that creativity resides, and the key to its development is to be found in the creative function of fantasy within emotional relationships. In the past, creative activities were encouraged as a safety-valve for repressed tendencies, for their therapeutic as well as purely educational benefits. Present-day knowledge carries the process a little further. Through play the child learns how to handle and direct his fantasy, and the therapeutic and educational processes are almost indistinguishable. If the child does not learn how to control his fantasy, his creative process will be stultified during his adult years. Children have more direct contact than adults with reverie and the world of imagination, and have a broad and flexible self-image. This self-concept is strongest when it can accept regression to primitive, naive and even taboo ideas, and yet assume a fairly advanced degree of rationality and self-criticism. The well-adjusted person realises that he can afford to allow regression because he is confident that he can correct himself. Freedom has reached an advanced stage when the capacity to control regression exists. A certain amount of tension, the natural result of mental conflict, can improve and intensify creative performance, and the proper aim of education is not to free individuals from tension, but to enable them to control it.

Whereas for most of the last century creativeness was thought to be the prerogative of a few geniuses (a very small minority of the population), since Sir Francis Galton initiated his study of individual differences (1869) more and more psychologists believe that creative potential resides in every individual and that creativity can be actualised at almost any age. Rogers (1959) proposed conditions of psychological safety which he believed would facilitate creativity in *all* students. These conditions were that the person should feel of substantial worth to himself and his peers, and that external criticism should be absent. If the teacher provided these conditions in the classroom, psychological freedom would prevail and the individual could express symbolically otherwise socially unacceptable behaviour. In these circumstances, a greater number of creatives would thrive than in conditions characterised by criticism and stern discipline.

Maslow (1959) held a similar view: he perceived creativity in every person, although in many this would remain as a suppressed potential, which would be released by a clearer understanding of the self. In his 'Self-Actualisation' theory, he asserted that when all other motives are satisfied, there are still problems a person seeks to solve, and this factor causes eternal self-actualisation. He pointed out that the creative persons he had studied were comparatively unfrightened by the unknown and indeed were attracted by it. The unknown element included the self, and so a clear self-image was essential in the creative process. Maslow claimed that where conditions of freedom and sympathy prevailed, creativity would emerge.

This emphasis on freedom was also central to the theory of Kubie (1958). He asserted that if any pupils were assisted to acquire divergent thinking attitudes, these would, in turn, free the pupils from fear neurosis and result in creativity.

This notion that all children possess the potential for creativity has also received support from recent developments in the mental measurement movement, which has indicated that the conventional conception of intelligence was formerly too narrow.

A number of theorists, particularly Guilford (1956), say there are at least 120 mental abilities, of which about half have been identified. These consist of *cognitive operations*—the processes of becoming aware; *memory operations*—retaining what has been cognised; *productive thinking processes*—convergent thinking where there is one accepted solution, and divergent thinking when possible solutions are many; and, finally, *evaluative processes*—when we assess what has been memorised, cognised, or produced. If intelligence is conceived as broadly as it should be, it must logically include these creative processes.

The genius stands out because he is extraordinarily well-endowed with creative abilities, and his ideas belong to the climate of the times in which he lives (*Zeitgeist*). But there are different degrees of genius. Variation is not confined to the eminently creative; it extends down through the population, the vast majority of which is inconspicuous in this respect. Whether or not a person is creatively productive, whether his creative potential reaches a point of fulfilment, depends on many circumstances —his upbringing, his external environment, his temperament, and not least his teachers.

Having established that creative potential exists, it must now be determined whether it can be deliberately developed, whether it can be 'taught'. As yet there is no comprehensive theory of instruction, but a number of interesting experiments seem to confirm that not only is it possible to develop creativity but also that this is eminently desirable.

Maslow's convincing argument is that suppressed creative potential can be released by means of a clearer understanding of the self, by a crystallisation of the self-image. His claim that creative people are attracted by the unknown was followed by the assertion that the vast majority of people reach a point where unavoidable mental conflict can either enhance or stultify creativity. The assumption is that people, especially the young, can and must be taught to use inner conflict beneficially.

Maltzman, Simon, Rachen and Licht (1960) claim that a person can be trained to produce original responses to given stimuli which have previously been undeveloped, and Paul Torrance's many studies on various aspects of creativity convinced him that children could be taught to bring their creative thinking abilities into use 'in acquiring even the traditional educational skills'.

Creative thinking can be fostered, but only when certain conditions are satisfied. Let us examine the characteristics of original thinkers, highly creative people whose work is accepted as original, individuals who have created something of distinctive beauty and worth, in order to see whether there are common characteristics which will point the way by which ordinary pupils, who constitute the majority of men, can be helped to develop creative thinking.

First, it is generally agreed that creative people have displayed a good deal of self-sufficiency. Anne Roe's most conclusive finding concerning the eminent scientists whom she studied (1953) was that they displayed a high degree of independence. She found that, when children, they pursued rather independent paths, playing with one or two close friends instead of a gang, and that they were very stubborn. Similar results were obtained by Barron (1957), who found original or creative people to be more independent than the ordinary; and Cattell and Drevdahl (1955) also discovered self-sufficiency to be a distinguishing trait among creative people. This view was again supported by Taylor and Holland (1962) who found creative persons more autonomous than others, more self-sufficient, more able to stand stress, and more independent in judgment.

Secondly, the vast majority of creative people have displayed indefatigable industry. Discoveries are made by what they know, not through some lucky chance. The inventor achieves novelty usually within the bounds of certainty. He finds when he is properly prepared for the finding. Notable composers such as Beethoven and Wagner mastered in their youth the existing rules of musical form and harmony. Many famous painters have begun by imitating assiduously other famous painters who have preceded them. It is vain to talk of inventiveness unless the inventor has mastered the tradition and basic skills of his field of study. Similarly, creativeness is highly unlikely unless the creator is equipped with the competence with which he can exhibit his creativeness. The thrill is almost impossible without the drill.

The Institute of Personality Assessment and Research (IPAR) was founded in 1949 at the University of California to discover more about human personality. Groups of people considered highly creative were invited to stay for the week-end in order to be questioned, tested, and observed; and attempts were made to compare them with other, less creative people in the same professional field. Over a number of years scientists, engineers, artists, writers and mathematicians have been carefully observed. What has impressed the researchers at IPAR is the dedication and quality of work produced by the creative individuals, their 'diligence, discipline and total commitment'.

Thirdly, creative ideas do not come without considerable thought about the problem or task. All the evidence points to the conclusion that in order to receive an inspiration the individual must first of all be intensely interested in the problem and have secured all the information he can get. The more skills and knowledge the individual has to draw upon the richer will be his product. Having mastered his craft the creative person is then likely to be challenged by a flash of insight or vision which usually arrives very unexpectedly. Writers, inventors and other creative workers invariably insist that creative ideas are not conscious products of previous thinking, but come spontaneously like a bolt from the blue, and particularly when the mind has let go and is thinking of something else. Newton's flash of inspiration about gravitation came with the falling of an apple; Darwin's insight into the theory of evolution arrived almost unexpectedly after years of gathering and arranging data. Bronowski described discoveries of science as 'explosions of hidden likeness', and the poet A. E. Housman described his inspiration in these words: 'There would flow into my mind with sudden and unaccountable emotion, sometimes a line or two of verse, sometimes a whole stanza.'

But even the poet, supposedly the most free of creators, is constrained by the known rules within which novelty can be expressed. The creative spirit of the poet must take into account the wealth of varieties of order, and, like all other creators, he must work tirelessly until the flesh of inspiration arrives. It is only then that his talent will bear fruit in the finished product.

Fourthly, creative people seem to have thrived upon and enjoyed disorder. Orderly routine and situations appear to have aroused their dislike. But behind this inclination to like and to construct what is not too simply ordered there appears to be a very strong need to achieve the most difficult and far-reaching orderliness. Barron's tests (1958) suggested that the subjects whom he studied remained independent and open to challenges presented by apparent imbalance and imperfection on the surface. He used mosaics and a number of Rorschach's blot tests, and the findings illustrated the creative response to disorder which seemed to find an elegant new order far more satisfying than any that could be evoked by a simpler configuration. The more creative of the subjects were more at home with the complexity of apparent disorder. They were ready to abandon old dissatisfactions for new possibilities. To the creative person, disorder offered the potential of a subtle order.

Fifthly, most creative people have displayed their creativity in one specialised field. Shelley would have been sadly out of place in Pasteur's laboratory, and Christopher Wren rather bewildered in Van Gogh's studio. Although there have been notable exceptions (for example, Leonardo da Vinci, Michelangelo, and Albert Schweitzer) who displayed their genius in a number of directions, the vast majority of creatives have concentrated on one. This is not unexpected because the industry required as a necessary preliminary to the creative product hardly allows a person in one lifetime to become familiar with the tradition and craft of more than one area of activity.

While the four characteristics of creative people—self-sufficiency, tremendous industry, unexpected flashes of insight, and specialisation—seem fairly constant, we cannot come to any obvious conclusions about the effect of social adjustment on creativity. Many brilliant and productive people have had marked social maladjustments. Van Gogh, Beethoven, and Jonathan Swift are well-known for their eccentricity and temperamental outbursts, but da Vinci, Brahms, Mendelssohn, Jefferson, Tennyson, and Browning displayed admirable social adjustment. We do not yet understand the relationship between adjustment and creativeness, but without the comfort of research it seems that neither social adjustment nor social maladjustment appear as a barrier to the creative process.

We should not assume that these characteristics are confined to the highly creative. We are all creative to some degree, and we should examine such characteristics for their implications in the creative process. It is not unreasonable to assume that the approaches of highly creative individuals can be of assistance to the vast majority of ordinary people to help them become more creative. Creativity varies in depth and scope rather than type.

A number of theorists have found evidence that various levels of creativity exist, and while nearly everyone participates in the lower levels, only the highly creative arrive at the upper levels.

The first level, according to Irving Taylor (1959) is the level of *expressive* creativity which involves spontaneous independent expression where the quality of the product is unimportant and in which there can be very little originality. The second level is that of *productive* creativity. At this stage there is a tendency to control free play and improve technique, but at this stage, too, the products may not be different from those of other people. In the third level, *inventive* creativity, invention and creativity are important characteristics which involve a perception of 'new and unusual relationships between previously separated parts'. The fourth level, the *innovative*, is found in a few people only. Here there is a modification of the basic foundation of a whole field of study in the arts or sciences. Only geniuses will work at the final *emergentative* level where the product emerges in its most fundamental and abstract form.

Most school-children can successfully move through the first two levels and, with good teaching and satisfactory motivation, can in time enter the third stage of the *inventive*. The vast majority will never produce at the *innovative* and *emergentative* grades, but even so their natural urge to create will have been satisfied and the quality of their work and indeed of their lives will be improved.

At all these levels except the first, the *expressive* level, the process of creative thought passes through three well-defined stages. The first of these stages is that of incubation.

A person begins to think creatively in very much the same way that he learns to read or write—by *doing* it. The pupil must be able to move through sets of ideas with fluency. At this early stage the creative work is to read, to discover and to explore. He must add to his fund of knowledge, and he must perfect his basic skills. The vast majority of innovators have been masters of the traditional method from which they departed. They have profited from what is already known because without it they could not tell what is new, or combine the older forms in a new pattern. Part of the work of this stage will be that of eliminating the trite and the ordinary. This first stage is for most people a long and painstaking one. There must be time to digest knowledge, to practise skills, time to feel challenged by a problem or idea, and time to mull it over before expressing it in the creator's characteristic medium.

The second is the illumination stage. At all levels of creativity, following a period of what can best be described as 'muddled suspense', there will be sudden and unexpected flashes of insight. A solution or a novel idea appears out of nowhere and often in the midst of some other activity, as in the case of Archimedes in his bath. Poincaré insisted that a period of preliminary conscious work always preceded fruitful unconscious work, and Bertrand Russell describes the frustration of trying to force a mathematical hypothesis to completion by sheer concentration before he discovered the necessity of 'waiting for it to find its own subconscious development'.

This spontaneous and almost involuntary creation is followed by conscious and rational effort in the third stage, that of reinforcement. The flashes of insight will not bear fruit as creative work without persistence, or what the famous mathematician Hadamard called 'a tenacious continuity of attention'. The solution which results from insight may not be *the* solution. Often the creative worker can see no apparent progress that might reward him. Many will give up and their creative potential will be wasted. The ability to create grows with practice and depends upon both the motivation and the intensity of the encounter with the subconscious. Spontaneous and involuntary production should foster a heightened degree of awareness which will enable the persevering individual to produce creative work. While the creative leap never takes exactly the same form twice, even for a particular individual, general characteristics are apparent.

The creative process comes from within and from without. It is by means of personal qualities, indefatigable industry, independence, patience and perseverance at various levels, and through definable stages, that the creative process seems to operate. This has many implications for the schools.

References

BARRON, F. 'The Psychology of Imagination'. *Scientific American*, **199**, 50, 1958 (151).

BARRON, F. 'Originality in Relation to Personality and Intellect'. *Journal of Personality*, **25**, 1957 (730–42).

CATTELL, R. B., and DREVDAHL, J. E. 'A Comparison of the Personality Profile of American Researchers with that of

Eminent Teachers and Administrators and the General Population'. *Journal of Educational Psychology*, **46**, 1955.

GALTON, F. *Hereditary Genius*. London: Collins, 1869.

GUILFORD, J. P. 'The Structure of Intellect'. *Psychological Bulletin*, **53**, 1956.

GUILFORD, J. P., and MERRIFIELD, D. R. 'The Structure of the Intellect Model'. *Reports* from the Psychology Laboratory, University of Southern California, 1966.

HADAMARD, J. *The Psychology of Invention in the Mathematical Field*. Princeton, N.J.: Princeton University Press, 1949.

KUBIE, L. *Neurotic Distortion in the Creative Process*. Lawrence, Kans.: University Press of Kansas, 1958.

MALTZMAN, I., *et al*. 'Experimental Studies on the Training of Originality'. *Psychological Monographs*, **74**, 1960 (74).

MASLOW, A. H. 'Creativity in Self-actualising People'. In ANDERSON, H. H. (ed.) *Creativity and its Cultivation*. New York: Harper, 1959.

PIAGET, J. *The Psychology of Intelligence*. New York: Harcourt, Brace, 1950.

POINCARÉ, H. (trans. Maitland, F.) *Science and Method*. New York: Dover, 1952.

ROE, A. 'A Psychological Study of Eminent Psychologists and Anthropologists and a Comparison with Biological and Physical Scientists'. *Psychological Monographs*, **67**, 352, 1953.

ROGERS, L. R. 'Toward a Theory of Creativity'. In ANDERSON, H. H. (ed.) *Creativity and its Cultivation*. New York: Harper,1959.

TAYLOR, C. W., and HOLLAND, J. L. 'Development and Applications of Tests of Creativity'. *Revue of Educational Research*, **32**, 1962.

TAYLOR, I. 'The Nature of the Creative Process'. In SMITH, D. (ed.) *An Examination of the Creative Process*. New York: Hastings House, 1959.

TORRANCE, E. P. *Education and the Creative Potential*. Minneapolis, Minn.: University of Minnesota Press, 1963.

Further Reading

BRONOWSKI, J. *Science and the Human Values*. New York: Harper, 1956.

CATTEL, R. B., and BUTCHER, H. J. *The Prediction of Achievement and Creativity*. Indianapolis, Ind.: Bobbs-Merrill, 1968.

CAUDWELL, H. *The Creative Impulse*. London: Macmillan, 1951.

COX, C. M. *Genetic Studies of Genius, Vol. 2: The Early Mental Traits of Three Hundred Geniuses*. Stanford, Calif.: Stanford University Press, 1926.

DREVDAHL, J. E., and CATTELL, R. B. 'Personality and Creativity in Artists and Writers'. *Journal of Clinical Psychology*, 14, 1958.

EISNER, E. W. 'A Typology of Creativity in the Visual Arts'. In BRITAIN, W. L. *Creativity and Art Education*. Washington, D.C.: National Art Education Association, 1964.

KNELLER, G. R. *The Art and Science of Creativity*. New York: Holt, Rinehart and Winston, 1965.

LANDIS, M. 'Creativity—a precious possession'. *Child Education*, **37,** 4, 1960.

LOVELL, K., and SHIELDS, J. B. 'Some Aspects of the Gifted Child'. *British Journal of Educational Psychology*, **37,** 1967.

STERN, K. *The Flight from Woman*. London: Allen and Unwin, 1965.

THURSTONE, L.L. 'Creative Talent'. In THURSTONE, L.L. (ed.) *Applications of Psychology*. New York: Harper, 1952.

WARREN, J. R., and HEIST, P. A. 'Personality Attributes of Gifted College Students'. *Science*, **CXXXII**, August 1960 (330–1).

CHAPTER THREE

Creativity and the Educator

The aims of any school must be to secure the full potential of its pupils in both body and mind, to ensure that these are used to the good of the community, and to give adequate preparation for everyday life in the world of work and leisure. It will not succeed in any one of these aims unless it offers a place for all kinds of creative work.

From our study of the creative process it is already evident that no single set of principles can be deduced which will ensure the success of creative work in the many facets of the work of the school. It is possible, however, to suggest a number of principles and issues for general consideration and for the guidance of teachers.

The atmosphere of our time, in general, militates against the fostering of creativeness in children. Where once fantasy and imagination were receiving full rein now, more and more, utility, realism and vocationalism are intruding into childhood experiences. Imaginative children's characters, such as Jack and his beanstalk, Tom Thumb, and the Wizard of Oz, are being gradually replaced by Fireman Fred and Mr Do-It-Yourself. Exciting adventures into the Land of Nod and the Enchanted Forest are making way for visits to local building sites and the Town Hall. Whereas first-hand experiences are vital in helping the child to come to terms with his environment, vicarious experiences are also necessary for the stimulation of his imagination.

In present-day school organisation the importance of group dynamics and the social and educational interaction of pupils needs to be underlined. The child regarded as most to be pitied is the isolate—usually the pupil who likes to be different in some way or other. The emphasis is indeed on convergence rather than on divergence. Whilst the group is a very important unit in modern learning, there are times, nevertheless, when the individual must be allowed to set himself his own peculiar problem, to work at his own pace and in his own way.

Few people can endure being a minority of one. Creativity often necessitates independence of mind and unusualness. Less creative workers seem more oriented towards quick achievement while more creative minds work more slowly at first, marshalling their resources (Stein, 1956). When an individual thinks in ways which are customarily taboo, he is often regarded as strange and sometimes even mentally unbalanced by his peers. Creatives often have the reputation of possessing wild or silly ideas; there is an element of playfulness about their attitude, and their products tend to be off the beaten track. It is inevitable that creative persons will experience many tensions and problems of adjustment. More often than not, creative pupils will be more difficult to get on with than their fellows, but it must be realised that their behaviour is caused by independence of thought and not by deliberation or malice.

In many areas teachers have to cope with large classes, culturally deprived children, and (increasingly) the children of immigrants. In such circumstances it is difficult to follow the interests and desires of each individual child. The constant learning of the basic skills and the new vocabulary necessary for cognitive development make it almost impossible to concentrate on anything but group teaching under these conditions.

Recent research shows the existence of considerable estrangement between highly creative pupils and their teachers (Getzels and Jackson, 1962; Torrance, 1962). Teachers are often far from enthusiastic about the child who is strikingly creative. Individualistic children with unconventional attitudes often worry teachers, who regard it as their chief responsibility to develop the traditional and the conventional (Mackinnon, 1962). Teachers' assessments of creativity will tend to correlate more highly with conventional intelligence tests than with scores on creativity tests. Lovell and Shields (1967) found a strong positive relationship between scores obtained on tests of logical thinking and teachers' ratings for originality, but there was no relationship between scores on the creativity tests and the originality ratings. Teachers, they said, seemed to think of originality in terms of reasoning ability rather than inventiveness or original ideas. If this feeling is general it is small wonder that, in the past, creative activities have been regarded as 'frills' to be undertaken when, and only when, what were considered to be basic processes had been mastered. In general, the curricula of schools at all levels of education have, until recent years, been designed to develop thinking abilities reflected in the traditional types of intelligence. This type of thinking is vital to the learning process, but parallel treatment must be given to creative thinking.

The main problem of the school will be to cope with both external and internal pressures. External pressures take the form of selection procedures, examination requirements, the expectation of parents and employers, and the public's suspicion of any school activities which do not seem to produce tangible and rapid results. Internal pressures are equally strong. The child will not wish to be unusual or different from his fellows, and the vast majority of teachers are successful products of an educational system designed to preserve the conventional and the traditional. There is a circular process at work here which makes it difficult for teachers who themselves succeeded by not being creative, or by appearing not to be creative, to foster that very quality in their pupils. To do this teachers may well have to risk granting the creative pupils more autonomy than has ever been considered proper before, and perhaps even to reward behaviour that fails to comply with what they have conventionally been prepared to reward. The question is, not whether highly creative or highly intelligent pupils should be given priority, but how can teachers help pupils of widely varying abilities? An important factor of democracy is respect for the individual and this implies the right of everyone to develop in his own way so long as that way is socially tolerable. The mistaken view that equality means uniformity has held up the progress of creative behaviour in society for far too long.

In order to encourage creative effort in children, the teacher must become a fully functioning personality. To do this he must himself participate in original thinking processes. He must endeavour to eliminate well-established patterns of conventional and negative thought and to develop a more active awareness of divergent learning experiences. There is also a need for the teacher to be flexible in his thinking and methods.

The teacher has to accept what the child does in order to enlarge the background out of which he does it, and to develop his skills. This will involve producing an atmosphere conducive to creative work, introducing problems with plenty of time for exploring them, encouraging critical questioning at all stages so that children can discover their own intrinsic creative ability, giving frequent practice in the use of the imagination, and devising methods by which creative work can be evaluated and rewarded.

The creative being does not emerge suddenly. His development is gradual and takes place only in an atmosphere which allows him to express himself. The teacher must refrain from forcing creative growth; rather must he create conditions which allow creative work to develop. The actual moment when a child is creative, and realises this—the creative leap—cannot be induced by the teacher, but must be allowed for, and is most likely to occur in a particular kind of setting. There must be no semblance of tyrannical authoritarianism in which spontaneity is denied, nor yet too much license causing uncertainty and distraction.

A wise teacher will provide a variety of aesthetic experiences. Listening to music, reading or being read to, looking at painting or sculpture may mould the separated elements of previous thinking into total insight. The child needs the support of the teacher in thinking and expressing ideas that are unconventional and unusual. The pupil must feel that he is not on trial as a person, and that activity, individuality and personal differences are valued. In contrast to the usual classroom situation, criticism must be postponed until after the actual production of ideas. Discrimination of the product is necessary, but the pupil must never be made to feel that, because his ideas are rejected, he is also rejected as a person. Hilgard and Sears (1964) showed a positive correlation between creativity and the demonstration by teachers of their willingness to listen often to the ideas of their pupils. In such an atmosphere children can permit themselves more leeway in the expression of unconventional ideas without fear of devastating or sarcastic criticism. This will, in turn, create an atmosphere in which pupils are more tolerant of unconventional ideas among themselves. Peer groups can exert considerable pressure on any child who is non-customary in thought and behaviour (Torrance, 1963). It would seem, therefore, that more self-competition and less competition between peers is what is needed.

If the appropriate atmosphere exists within the school and within the classroom, the child's fears and aggressions will decrease, confidence will develop, and with it security and a feeling

B

of self-satisfaction with regard to his individuality. But teaching a child to think creatively means more than providing the appropriate conditions for thinking. It means identifying the specific skills involved in creating and deliberately teaching these: not merely tolerating divergence, but encouraging it.

Teachers can help children in detecting new problems, in thinking of diverse and novel modifications to traditional ideas, and in improvising situations calling for resource. Children vary in their sensitivity to problems, and since awareness of a gap or problem is often the first step towards creativity, teachers must help their pupils to detect their problems. Ordinarily, children cannot be expected to produce original ideas until trite and ordinary thoughts are eliminated (Maltzman, 1960). Problem-finding must precede problem-solving, and the teacher's support and sympathy is most effective at the beginning of problem solving experiences. Like the human being who produces it, the creative idea is weakest at birth.

After encouraging this sensitivity to problems, the child must be given considerable experience in problem solving. Many problematic situations can be presented which will extend the child's ingenuity in imaginative situations. Some questions which might be posed are: 'What could happen if it were cold every summer and warm every winter?' 'How can you open a tin without a tin opener?' 'How could you sleep comfortably if there were no such thing as a bed?' 'How could you make a fire without matches?' 'If you were exposed to extreme cold, what would you do to comfort yourself?' 'How many ways can a fire be started?'

An individual is problem-solving when he sees new ways of attaining a goal, when he has to adapt his previous learning to new situations, and when he acquires a new pattern of responses. A clearer conception of the character of the goal to be attained is essential because without it the problem-solver cannot select out of his previous experience the appropriate means to attain the goal. Some problems may be attacked individually or in a group. The co-operative effort of a group working on a problem can be beneficial to every individual in the group, particularly if the group has a genuine problem, one which, in the course of their work, they have found necessary and desirable to solve. When they feel that they have a choice in the posing of a problem, they will accept responsibility for its solution.

The school contributes to the development of problem-solving in a number of ways. It is the school environment which provides the background of understanding, information and skills essential to both the posing and solution of problems. It is the school that helped to create the problem situation by arousing the child's curiosity. The school also is responsible for stimulating and utilizing the child's interests, thus placing him in a situation which makes problem-solving probable. It is the school, too, that encourages the child to make and test hypotheses and to develop the necessary skills in this respect. Problem-solving behaviour will be developed if problems are the central concern of the learning experiences provided in a school, and if the acquisition of knowledge, skills and understanding are made relevant to the solution of problems of genuine significance to the child.

One development in this respect in the U.S.A. is described as 'brain-storming' (not to be confused with 'brain-washing'). This approach was developed by Alex Osborn (1957) and widely used in some parts of America. The basic notion is that a group of people together are able to express aloud ideas about a given topic as these come into their minds, without fear of contradiction or criticism. The advocates of this method claim that a kind of chain reaction will result and produce a far greater harvest of ideas than would be possible for individuals to produce by themselves. Further, they claim that this free flow of ideas and associations will help the individuals who take part in it to become more divergent in their thinking. The value of brain-storming is still the subject of research and some of the findings have been conflicting. A study by Donald Taylor and others in Yale University suggested that brain-storming would inhibit problem-solving, and other criticisms have been made by Parnes and Meadow (1963) at the University of Buffalo.

Lateral thinking, publicised by Edward de Bono (1967), is a process of thought used in problem-solving. The basic principles are recognition of dominant ideas, a relaxation of the rigid control of traditional (vertical) thinking, a concentrated search for different ways of looking at things, and use of choice. The lateral thinker does not achieve results by step-by-step logical method, and is more concerned with reaching a solution than with being right or wrong. Lateral thinking can be developed by practice and may well be an aid to creativity.

It is evident that until more research clarifies the situation, schools must approach such methods with caution. It is probable that children will solve creative problems less successfully by being put in a situation where creative notions are expected of them by their group than if they arise naturally from their everyday work. A situation where children are spoon-fed, in that ready-made solutions are constantly available, will deprive them of opportunities to grow creatively.

It has been agreed by researchers and teachers that children learn best what comes to them pleasantly and as a personal discovery. It has become the teacher's duty to create an environment in which the children can progress and situations in which they learn to learn.

The accent on discovery is particularly emphasised where mathematical, scientific and linguistic concepts are being introduced to children in novel ways, involving the direct participation of the children themselves. A child works at a task because there is something inherent in it which holds his attention. The direct experiences that he enjoys should be controlled because they give direction to learning, yet still provide for and encourage individual creative work within a prescribed field of study.

In a good school the child will be roused to ask questions by some story or some event in his own environment. He will be directed towards finding the answers for himself, and, if it is anything but a fleeting interest, that child will then write, model, plan, exhibit, or lecture to his group or class on his findings.

There must be areas of instruction in which opportunities are provided for discovery as well as remembering. There must be provision of time for the consideration of facts as well as for repeating them. The children must be taught that a problem may have several different interpretations and solutions. The teacher must help pupils to discover their strengths and give them opportunities to experiment and to try out various ways of developing their abilities.

For discovery to take place on a large scale within a school there must be a modification of the traditional organisation of the curriculum into subjects. Subjects are human creations and the children are not in school merely to learn of other people's creative work, but to produce their own. An over-emphasis on learning by subjects reflects a dated and over-compartmentalised system out of touch with mid-twentieth-century thinking. While major scientific and technical experiences shade off into each other, it is rather absurd to pigeonhole learning experience in this way. Of course, subjects integrate themselves up to a point, but in too restricted and too inflexible a manner. An over-emphasis on subjects distorts experience because it focuses on a narrow segment of real life at a high level of abstraction. In real situations, questions leap subject barriers. Integration involves increasing flexibility both of groups and of the curriculum. Activities involving problem-solving and discovery will more beneficially take place in a situation which is not too restricted by organisation or by time-table, and yet in which there is order and routine acceptable to the pupils, whether they are working individually or in a group.

Children learn by doing, and doing is in itself an indispensible basis for imaginative thought. Imagination is least controlled in childhood and then has not had time to decline through lack of use. When the child learns that he can manipulate past experiences by recalling and rearranging them, he has begun to use his imagination. It is imperative that the school encourages development of the imagination, for it has many functions to perform.

Even the best-adjusted person has a considerable number of frustrations. Imaginative action is the means by which a child can satisfy his inadequacies. Because of the new ideas and situations which confront him, a child's imaginings may be full of fear, and he will need support, usually from a sympathetic adult, in order to learn to enjoy the thrill of ideational danger. Imagination, therefore, satisfies the child's appetite for change and gratifies the challenge of the unknown.

Imagination also provides a means for children to explore social relationships and to communicate and to share emotion. The fact that the experience is individual, that the child's thoughts are his own, will satisfy his need for self-mastery and assertion. If a child is unable to find a rational explanation, he calls imagination to his aid. It provides the essential means for the child to continue experimenting despite the obstacle of rational explanation which would otherwise be unbearable.

Apart from the obvious benefit of skill and muscular control which imagination can develop if skilfully applied to physical play and movement, it can also be an important factor in the development of concentration. Frequent imaginative play in which sustained absorption takes place will inevitably extend the child's power to concentrate on a task if that task is sustained by interest.

The imagination will also foster a widening of interests because it knows no boundaries. It can wander not only in the known world but into space, into history, and into non-reality. But it is also, to some extent, controlled by reality. One can only imagine in proportion to what one already knows. Therefore imagination is not only limited by knowledge, it can also establish a thirst for more knowledge.

It is easier to impede than to encourage imagination. A rigid goal or model, or ridicule, or sarcasm, can discourage the process. A sterile environment can also be a considerable obstacle to imagination, because it reduces the number of past and significant experiences.

How can a school foster imagination and capitalise on it, to aid creative learning? Its starting point must be activity. Like the body and the mind, imagination must be exercised; it must have constant and not merely sporadic use. During the infant stage, when imagination, fantasy and memory are inter-mingled, the school must let children play out their fantasies. For this they can identify themselves with fairies, witches, gnomes, or any other creature, good or bad. Part of the infant teacher's work, however, will be to encourage the children to use their imagination more in real situations—such as a 'shop', 'house', 'hospital', or any situation reasonably well-known to them. At later stages of schooling the child must be given further opportunities to develop his imagination untrammelled by rigid rules of taste and cultural pattern. Since imagination is based on the development of use and meaning, it is important to provide the child with tangible opportunities of learning, first about his environment, and then about the world at large. There must, nevertheless, at this stage be plenty of opportunity for the pupil's imagination to enjoy carefree exploration. Imagining 'Under the Sea', for example, will have close affinity with a consideration of marine biology.

Teachers of both young and older children need above all to cultivate within themselves a sense of wonder and mystery. They must attempt to look at the world through the eyes of a child. The tempo of life in the second half of the twentieth century has caused us to take many things for granted. Our senses have become dull and we have ceased to wonder. Teachers, in particular, must endeavour to share rich experiences with children—the beauty of a landscape, a flower, or a snowflake, the majesty and force of lightning flashes or sea waves at high tide, the mystery of the insight of a poet or prophet. We must regard imagination less as the means to devise something new than as an ability to reveal as new that which already exists.

Research tells us that both children and adults develop along those lines which they find rewarding. If schools are to develop the creative thinking abilities of children they must find ways of rewarding this kind of achievement and not confine their applause to thinking that merely conforms.

Success is vital if a learner is to persist. While there is no conclusive experimental evidence on the virtues of reward and punishment in learning, experienced teachers will have no doubt that more is to be gained by rewarding achievement than by punishing mistakes. Where considerations of success predominate there are more chances of redeeming failure. Spaulding (1963) found that the quality of creative expression in primary school children deteriorated when teachers used shame as a punishment-technique in formal group instruction.

Special care must be taken when a consideration of rewarding creative thinking and work takes place. Creativity is finely balanced and children whose creative thoughts may be different from those of others, or of their peer-group, will need support and confirmation by the teacher if they are going to allow themselves creative thoughts again. The teacher has a paramount contribution to make by rewarding divergent thinking with praise, by being respectful if unusual questions are asked, by being tolerant of ambiguity, and by allowing a considerable amount of practice which is not criticised or assessed.

The complete creative performance must, of necessity, include evaluation of the results. This may be at the level of self-evaluation, through discussion and communication of ideas, among pupils or between teacher and pupil, and through an assessment by the teacher of the finished creative product. But evaluation is often best suspended until ideas are well developed. Children should be taught the value of their work and how to apply their critical thinking after the production of these thoughts rather than before.

The schools are responsible for the conditions and experiences that make up the child's life during school hours. But parents assume this responsibility when the child is at home. The parent-controlled part of each day affords significant learning experiences for the child and carries expectancies for certain kinds of attitudes and actions.

Contact between parents and teachers needs to be a two-way process, from home to school and from school to home. Inadequate communication between the two may considerably hinder the scholastic progress of the child. This is especially true when considering creative work. The teacher must act as interpreter of the child's work to his parents, who can mistakenly stifle creative growth through imposing adult standards and ideas on him and attempting to correct anything which does not conform to a conventional standard. This contact must be maintained in parent–teacher associations, open days, school visits, home visits, planned home-school conferences, and study groups.

In frequent meetings, the teacher should assist the parents to extend the creative experiences of their children by discussion, experimenting, discovering and constructing, by being tolerant of divergent ideas, by sometimes answering the child's questions in a factual manner, but at other times guiding the child to investigate in order to discover answers for himself, and by sharing stimulating experiences with him.

The essential characteristic of creative work in schools is that every pupil will have the opportunity to create in thought, movement, arrangement, and construction, in a variety of media and materials, something that arises from within himself and is characteristic of him. Creative teaching arouses a zeal for learning, and stimulates selective thinking and purposeful action. It proceeds with the conviction that there are within each person impulses which need to be encouraged and nurtured. The important thing is that the child, from within himself and working in his own way, has produced something of which he can approve.

The school cannot create creativity, but it can do much to encourage and develop it. Its prime aim is to enable each child to find himself, to test out his unique thoughts, and to have his uniqueness accepted by his teachers and peers. When the pupil is guided in expressing his abilities in such a way that his own creative self is not blocked, learning will be satisfying, beneficial, and pleasant.

References

DE BONO, E. *The Use of Lateral Thinking*. London: Cape, 1967.
GETZELS, J. W., and JACKSON, P. W. *Creativity and Intelligence*. New York: John Wiley, 1962.
HILGARD, E. R., and SEARS, P. S. 'The Teacher's Role in the Motivation of the Learner'. In *Theories of Learning and Instruction* (63rd N.S.S.E. Yearbook). Chicago, Ill.: University of Chicago Press, 1964.
LOVELL, K., and SHIELDS, J. B. 'Some Aspects of the Gifted Child'. *British Journal of Educational Psychology*, 37, 1967.
MACKINNON, D. W. 'The Nature and Nurture of Creative Talent'. *American Psychologist*, 17, 1962.
MALTZMAN, I., *et al.* 'Experimental Studies on the Training of Originality'. *Psychological Monographs*, LXXIV, 6, 1960.
OSBORN, A. F. *Applied Imagination*. New York: Scribner, 1957.
PARNES, S. J., and MEADOW, A. 'Development of Individual Creative Talent'. In BARRON, C. W., and BARRON, F. (eds.) *Scientific Creativity: Its Recognition and Development*. New York: John Wiley, 1963.
SPAULDING, R. *Achievement, Creativity and Self-concept Correlates of Teacher-pupil Transaction in Elementary Schools*. Urbana, Ill.: University of Illinois Press, 1963.
STEIN, M. I. 'A Transactional Approach to Creativity'. In TAYLOR, C. W. (ed.), *The 1955 University of Utah Conference on the Identification of Creative Scientific Talent*. Salt Lake City, Utah: University of Utah Press, 1956.
TAYLOR, C. W., BERRY, P. C., and BLOCK, C. H. 'Does Group Participation when using Brain Storming facilitate or inhibit Creative Thinking?' New Haven, Conn.: Yale University Indust. Admin. Psych., 1957.
TORRANCE, E. P. *Guiding Creative Talent*. Englewood Cliffs, N.J.: Prentice-Hall, 1962.
TORRANCE, E. P. *Education and the Creative Potential*. Minneapolis, Minn.: University of Minnesota Press, 1963.

Further Reading

ANDERSON, H. H. (ed). *Creativity and Cultivation*. New York: Harper, 1959.
ASCH, S. 'Opinions and Social Pressures'. *Scientific American*, 199, 3, 1958.

BUGELSKI, B. R. *The Psychology of Learning.* New York: Holt, Rinehart and Winston, 1960.

GRUBER, H. E. (ed.) *Contemporary Approaches to Creative Thinking.* New York: Atherton, 1962.

GUILFORD, J. P. 'Factors that Aid and Hinder Creativity'. *Teacher's College Record,* **LXIII**, 1962.

MEDNICK, S. *Learning.* Englewood Cliffs, N. J.: Prentice-Hall, 1964.

PARNES, S. J., and HARDING, H. F. *A Source Book for Creative Teaching.* New York: Scribner, 1962.

RAZIK, A. *Creativity Studies and Related Areas.* Albany, N.Y.: State University of New York Press. 1965.

SEARS, P. 'Levels of Aspirations in Academically Successful and Unsuccessful Children'. *Journal of Abnormal and Social Psychology,* 35, 1940 (498).

SKINNER, B. F. 'The Science of Learning and the Art of Teaching'. *Harvard Education Review,* **24,** 2, 1954.

STEIN, M. I., and HEINZE, S. J. *Creativity and the Individual.* New York: Free Press, 1960.

TAYLOT, C. W. (ed.) *Widening Horizons in Creativity.* New York: John Wiley, 1964.

TROW, W. C. *Teacher and Technology.* New York: Appleton-Century-Crofts, 1963.

WILLIAMS, F. E. 'Teaching for Creative Thinking'. *The Instructor,* **76**, May 1967.

CHAPTER FOUR

Creativity in the Curriculum

There is much emphasis in many of today's schools on work appealing to the child's curiosity and on permitting him to discover knowledge for himself. There has been a welcome reaction against the system in which pupils were desk-bound and drilled into becoming passive recipients of knowledge. But it is imperative that all teachers and educationists should realise the folly of regarding newer approaches as being sufficient in themselves. The task of the schools is to guide children so that they delight in creating things in their own way. That happy state of affairs will never be attained if standards are neglected and if practice and thorough learning of the basic skills are denied.

New provisions do not necessarily constitute innovation. The cycle of fashion can indeed have harmful effects if evaluation and assessment are absent. Not everything new is good. Any new aspect should be more intelligible, self-motivating and purposeful than that which it replaced, and it is valueless for a child to discover new knowledge if he quickly forgets what he has discovered. Children delight in making new movements, but they also have pleasure in repeating old ones. Before they are able to explore the unknown, they must consolidate the known.

Because the child can create only out of his own experience and feelings, a considerable background of solid knowledge must be acquired before he can diverge into individualistic productive work. Only when the meaning of words can be discriminated precisely can the child grow in the power to think, to reason, and to produce creative work. The work of a number of theorists, particularly that of Basil Bernstein, has shown that the majority of children come from homes which have a poor linguistic background, and are severely handicapped, not only in verbal expression, but also in abstract concept formation—the essential basis for creative work. Teachers must become more aware of non-verbal modes of communication and thinking which pro-provide culturally handicapped children with alternative response modes that lead to creative problem-solving (Riessman, 1962).

Almost every human activity possesses both a creative and a technical aspect. The one will enable the performer to evaluate the quality of his product; the other will provide him with the technique necessary to produce the product. The young child, for example, may wish to paint a picture of a horse, but to do so he must be able to hold and control the brush. He needs also the ability to perceive different kinds of lines, curved and straight, which constitute the outline of the horse, and the manipulative skill to mix the paint and move the brush across the paper in the required way. The resulting picture will be the child's version of a horse, but his creativity could not have been expressed without the technique of painting and without the knowledge of what a horse looks like. There is nothing more frustrating to a child than wanting to express himself verbally, or with malleable material, or on paper, without having the necessary means to do so to his own satisfaction.

Although in the past the emphasis on technique far outweighed that on creativity, it is important, during the swing to more modern methods, that the opposite error of underestimating the importance of technique is not committed. What is needed is to secure the balance between the two.

Often children will be exercised in the mastery of skills before the enthusiasm for creative work is kindled. Many activities have to be savoured before satisfaction in these activities can be experienced. Teachers must allow plenty of time for a child to learn and to develop attitudes and goals. A creative outlook must be gradual because what is needed is growth, not transplantation.

Not only must the teacher have a conscious recognition that time is required for the development of creative work, but he needs also to distinguish between individuality and laziness, between self-sufficiency and morbid withdrawal, between the creative pupil and the merely superficial worker, the individualist and the exhibitionist.

There is a danger in regarding originality, spontaneity and freedom as the only worthy ends in education. Genuine feelings can also be expressed within a framework as well as outside it. Comformity and control also have their virtues. Self-control and self-sacrifice are as important as self-expression and self-assertion. There are many occasions when the non-conformer must be kept within such limits as are necessary for the well-being of the remainder of the pupils. There is no evidence to show that the security of the classroom situation blunts the edge of creativity of pupils of any age range.

Before creativity is possible, the first steps should be made towards acquiring the techniques of a skill, using suitably simple material. Sufficient repeated practice should take place in order to allow both confidence and familiarity to grow. This practice should be closely related to the learner's motivation and his interests.

When the basics of a skill are mastered, the teacher's training must gradually develop the child's independence. Mechanical work will slowly give way to work based on genuine understanding and interest. Then the learner uses his skill for personal enrichment under the sympathetic guidance of the teacher. As the pupil develops, his expression will acquire a creative and satisfying form. This, in turn, may well inspire a demand for further advance in technique. Whereas in the early stages of acquiring creativity, discipline comes from outside the learner, during the later refined stages of expression it comes from within the learner, and is self-disciplined. At first it was a state of affairs, now it has become a state of mind.

We must now turn our attention to various areas of the curriculum. The names of the subjects which appear on school timetables, or on schemes of work where timetables do not exist, the grouping by which learning takes place, the arrangement of the school day and ways of teaching, all differ from school to school. But in every school the children's education includes listening, speaking, and expressing themselves in language, mathematical work, knowledge of their environment, near and far, past and present, expressive work with materials, and movement. In nursery and infant schools learning is, for the most part, undifferentiated: reading, writing, mathematics, crafts, art, and listening to stories go on more or less together. Unclassified education of this kind continues in a number of junior schools, but many are still organised in more conventional and traditional forms. Nevertheless there is a growing tendency for projects, topics and centres of activity to cut across subject barriers and re-utilise knowledge and skills from many sources. In all but a few secondary schools, which are fettered by examination syllabuses, clearly defined categories of learning prevail. Even here, experiments in team-teaching, leisure training and work experience are helping to merge a number of areas of learning.

The curriculum is constantly under review by administrators, by members of the public, and especially by teachers who, in well-established in-service training and teachers' centres, are becoming important participants in the process of curriculum review. There is a continuous change in emphasis and scope and response to the fresh demands which the changing society and new knowledge make upon it. The Schools Council (Schools Council for the Curriculum and Examinations) was set up in 1964 to keep under review the curricula and teaching methods in primary and secondary schools, including aspects of school organisation. The three curriculum steering committees cover the age ranges 2–13, 11–16, and over 14, and ten separate committees look after mathematics, science, modern languages, English, Welsh, history, geography, religious instruction, classics, and technical and engineering studies. Serving school teachers are in a majority on all these committees.

The curriculum, stated in terms of subjects or activities or items in a syllabus, omits what teachers would regard as fundamental in the training they offer, such as the development of character qualities, of values and standards, and the development of pupils as persons. If creative learning is to be achieved, there must be active and sincere respect for each child at all times. There must be genuine acceptance and expectation of the fact that every child is unique. It is important that the teacher understands every child in his care in order to teach him in group situations. Valuing his own individuality in the freedom given to him, often in choice of activity and methods. the successful teacher comes to know every one of his pupils as individuals. No one area of learning can be omitted from the creative approach.

In the sections that follow, every well-established discipline in the ordinary curriculum of British schools today is examined in turn in order to consider the activities or procedures which might offer scope to the creative potential of children. Then some consideration will be given to the organisation of the curriculum and teacher-training. With regard to the conservative world of practical teaching, the conventional disciplines are considered separately, but it must be emphasised strongly that they merge and overlap. In the same way, attention is given to the *infant*, *junior* and *secondary* stages of schooling, although there is a significant movement towards lower, middle and upper schooling in a number of areas. Many different groupings and combinations, of both subjects and organisation, are possible, and different schools will interpret the various suggestions in ways best suited to their own circumstances. An attempt will be made to apply the principles of creative learning, in practical ways, not just to introduce novelty, but to help to make work already attempted in schools more imaginative, enlightened and creative.

Creativity must always be associated with happiness, whatever the quality of the product produced. There is much room for experimentation, for original thinking, for enterprise, and for adventure in all areas of the curriculum and in all school experience.

The Language Arts

The development of language is closely related to other aspects of child growth. The child participates in listening, speaking, reading, and writing at school and at home. Without language it is impossible to teach any other subject, and the teacher's programme must include training in speech, in reading, and in writing. The key to all three is understanding.

In the past there has been a great deal of dependence in schools upon the mechanical memorising of material and upon arid and irrelevant exercises. The result was stilted recitation, barking at print, parrot-like play-reading and stereotyped compositions. Because of the swing away from teaching formal English to a more free approach, much attention and publicity has been recently given to creative writing. In a sense, most writing was creative and the best work done in the schools of the past was creative in its true sense. As so often happens when a label is honoured with almost wholesale adaptation and allegiance, much ambiguity and not a little artificial and superficial work will result. It is necessary, therefore, to examine this label in some detail.

Creative Writing

Although the term 'composition' has unfortunate associations, it does contain the essential ingredient of creativity if regarded as an activity and not a subject. At worst, composition can be the most exacting, frustrating and dull exercise in the school week; at its best it can be rewarding, exciting, and creative. Free directed practice must banish the shadow of the old repressive discipline which often hides behind the label of creative writing.

The change to a freer writing, although it carries with it attendant dangers, is to be welcomed. In a world of rules and order, ways of escape are often necessary, especially for children. Make-believe based on fantasy is an important part of their world. The conventional world of adults is often puzzling, and although eventually children must abide by the traditional rules of society, in their imagination they frequently enjoy a release from the conventional world. Writing can provide this escape for them.

Creative writing has come to mean many things to numerous people, and it is important to have a clear notion of what it implies. The resulting product must be different, to some extent, from the commonplace and the ordinary. It will arise from the writer's desire to express himself, and will be original in that it is based on the child's own thoughts and feelings. We can perhaps define creative writing in this way: *a piece of spontaneous self-expression involving the writer's thoughts, imagination and feelings.*

Before the young writer can reach the relatively advanced stage of being able to put his thoughts on paper, he must have considerable help and guidance. The material is a transmutation of the child's own experience, and therein lies the chief difficulty. The majority of pupils have very little experience, and much even of this tends to sink quickly into the sub-conscious and can be evoked only with careful and skilful probing. It is only when the meanings of words are correctly distinguished that children can reason with sufficient clarity to enable them to put their thoughts on paper.

It is futile to believe that if teachers provide the opportunity to write, then ideas will come to children freely, and they will acquire naturally the technique which enables them to convey thoughts in writing. Adults, even teachers, would find considerable difficulty in writing creatively under such circumstances. The teacher has a significant role in encouraging worth-while responses from his pupils. In a freer approach, his responsibility is not diminished. Indeed, he must display more sympathy, intuition and involvement. He must guide his pupils in expanding and understanding their experience, and then, by appealing to their emotions and feelings, motivate such enthusiasm that they will welcome the opportunity to record these in writing.

If the teacher is not actively involved in enabling the child to express his experience and imagination, he may well be retarding linguistic progress and reinforcing inferior language habits. The researches of Bernstein (1961) in England, and Deutsch, Fantini and Weinstein (1968) and others in the United States, have shown convincingly that the majority of children of working-class parents have a restricted linguistic code. Young children possess a basic vocabulary and speech patterns derived mainly from language heard at home. It is apparent, therefore, that most of those from culturally deprived backgrounds will write in a restricted code, and for many of them the value of unrestricted freedom in writing is questionable. While it is necessary for them to have scope for their imagination, unless there is a continuing conscious attempt to improve standards of speech, vocabulary, and attendant facility in thought processes, there is a danger that these children will continue in relative linguistic backwardness. The teacher's first task with children who clearly suffer from a cultural handicap is to orientate them to a more elaborate linguistic code, so that they can express their thoughts in a precise, and later in a creative, manner.

Many important forms of expressive writing exist in addition to the imaginative, and these not only supplement the work directed to creative expression but can be considered as important preparations for it. The child, during the course of his school work, should have the opportunity of writing letters, real and imaginary, reports of incidents or club meetings, descriptions of all kinds of objects, and book and news reviews. Relevance to the present is as important as (some would say more important than) scope for the imagination. If the work, whatever its nature, bears the individual mark of the writer, and is the product of his own opinions and research, then it has every claim to be called creative.

Before examining the techniques and principles involved in acquiring creative writing, it is important to have a clear view of what we are hoping to achieve. While the ultimate aims of creative writing can never be narrowly defined, we are, nevertheless, clearly attempting to give the child scope to express himself in a way which is self-satisfying, and to give him a sense of fitness in language which will enable him not only to express and appreciate his own writing but also subsequently to appreciate the writing of others, thus opening the way for his fuller enjoyment of the riches of literature.

If these two aims are to be achieved, it must be realised that only a child with ideas can write creatively, and it is only through active personal experience, through the teacher, or through books, that he will acquire these ideas. The old form of preparation is not sufficient, especially if it is concerned mainly with mechanics and planning. The preparatory work must essentially be motivational —an inspiration to the child to feel, to think, and then to express his thoughts satisfactorily. Originality to any definite degree must not be expected in the early stages, but very soon, given the right stimuli, many children will reveal a natural and individual sensitivity for words.

Not only must teachers provide a whole range of direct experiences, but they must also provide challenge and stimulation so that these experiences acquire significance. Reading, discussion and discovery-work all synthesise ideas and bring to the surface relevant past experience. The enrichment of the child's written expression can take place in a number of ways.

The teacher, in reading to his pupils selected pieces of prose and poetry, and in encouraging selective reading on their parts, establishes a fund of experience and vocabulary from which they can draw when writing. If a careful selection of material is made, the teacher will provide a setting, create a situation, and conjure up a mood which will make children want to write and form a common pool of impressions to prepare for future work.

Teachers should always have available poems, prose extracts, suitable paintings, pictures of sculpture and architecture and recorded music to heighten the mood and stimulate the desire to write.

A number of excellent poem anthologies are available at both primary and secondary levels. *Come Follow Me* published by Evans Brothers and A. A. Milne's *When We were Very Young* and *Now we are Six* are particularly valuable for infant and lower juniors, while for the 10–12 age group Wollman and Grugeon's collection entitled *Happenings* published by Harrap have a fund of interesting poems. At secondary level John Wain's *Anthology of Modern Poets* (Hutchinson, 1963) and Ted Hughes' *Here Today* (Hutchinson, 1962) provide interesting and varied collections of stimulating poetry.

Catherine Storr, Modwena Sedgwick, Beatrix Potter, Philippa

Pearce and Ursula Williams have written many excellent and appealing stories in prose to appeal to primary school children, while at secondary level the work of Alan Garner, J. R. R. Tolkein, Leon Garfield, Graham Greene and William Mayne afford absorbing material.

The children's response to such writing may take many forms —stories, descriptions, talks, autobiographies, articles for class or school newspapers, and pieces of writing undertaken purely for enjoyment.

Another very popular method of stimulation is to invite children to listen to music chosen for its story or descriptive potential. It must be emphasised that to ask most children to write something at length after listening to music, if they are not accustomed to this procedure, is to give them a task which even teachers would find very difficult. But given the right atmosphere, a gradual introduction of this approach can result in very interesting work. The music must be carefully selected and must clearly evoke a mood or picture. Some of the work of Bach, Beethoven, Wagner, Kodaly, and Tchaikovsky is eminently suitable for this purpose, and the more modern music of Duke Ellington, Acker Bilk, Gershwin, and Rogers and Hart can be used with excellent results.

Examples from a mixed-ability class of ten-year-olds at Pwllhelli, North Wales, produced a wide variety of interpretations after hearing the 1812 Overture on two occasions and having had also an outline of the historical background to the composition. 'I dread to think of the dead men and blood on the battle field. The Anthem is being played. It is surely over.' (A relieved ending by Mary, aged 9.) 'We shall have silence now for those who died. They shall be remembered.' (Echoes of Armistice by Ian, aged 10.) 'After the battle my soldier husband lay in bed. Dead? A few days later he got better. Ever since we have lived happily and no more battles.' (Happy ending from Carol, aged 10.) 'We had won the bloody battle, and all the left men returned to their homes. We buried the dead, and quickly repaired the damage.' (Matter of fact ending by Gordon, aged 9.) 'Then my husband suddenly gave a cry of pain and died. I am not lonely because I have married my husband's best friend, Kerk. Sometimes I ask my husband what he thought of him, and what they did together.' (An unusual, not entirely happy, ending from Mary, aged 10.)

After listening to a record of Bach's 'Air on the G String' a
nine-year-old girl wrote this poem.

It is a sad song
A ship on the sea
A kind of gentle music
Like slow motion
Like a flowing river
Music for ice skating
Soft music
Crying music
As if everything is dying
As if the world has ended.

Further stimulation can be provided by showing children copies
of works of art, sculpture, and architecture. These can be acquired
at reasonable cost, or on loan from art galleries and libraries, or
on slides available from a number of firms. Children appreciate
the creative fantasies of artists like Hieronymus Bosch, Hokusai
and Klee, though most seem to prefer the splashed light and colour
of the Impressionists to the sombre tones of Rembrandt. They
marvel at the realism achieved by the artist who illustrates a current interest. The animal lover adores Durer's 'Hare', or Stubbs's
horses, and some boys, in particular, are excited by Goya's more
violent works. The average child is more amenable to pop art
than the average adult and this comparatively recent art form has
been represented in collage on many children's bedroom and
classroom walls. An abundance of well-chosen examples of paintings, drawing, sculpture, and design are contained in J. and G.
Grigson's *Shapes and Stories* (John Baker, 1964), A. E. Chases's
Famous Artists of the Past: A young People's Guide to Great Masters
(Macdonald, 1964), Bryan Holme's *Looking at Drawings* (Studio
Vista, 1966), and C. and M. Maclean's *Looking at Pictures* (Purnell,
1970). Not all the examples need be provided by well-known
artists and sculptors. Coloured pictures and illustrations are easily
obtained from numerous magazines and are useful sources of
inspiration.

Whatever means of stimulation are used, it is necessary to
develop in children a pleasure and confidence in using words to
their most effective purpose. From the first they will have learned
to distinguish between words in categories familiar to them, such
as 'big', 'huge', and 'gigantic'. They will then progress to words

associated with the senses, particularly those of touch, taste, and smell, and the sensations that these evoke. The progression then is to words carrying abstract ideas, best approached through the impact of familiar, personal feelings such as sadness, happiness, love and hate. The children should be given constant opportunities of looking, listening, and touching, and, where appropriate, smelling and tasting. Teachers must ensure many varieties of experience, actual and imaginary, if they are to bring liveliness and meaning to the words children write.

Equal in importance to enriched experience and effective stimulation is the provision of an informal and relaxed classroom atmosphere. Children should not be hampered by fears about their handwriting, grammar, and spelling, important as these are. A feeling of freedom is essential if the creative process is going to take place, but there has been too much vagueness about the connection between grammar, punctuation, spelling, and creative writing. It is evident that, at both primary and secondary levels, a systematised pattern of language usage must be established. Many teachers argue that random and incidental writing is value-less unless there is also directed practice in grammar, punctuation and spelling. Too often these are 'taught' in the hope that practice in isolated context will transfer to real writing. Experience and the little research that is available seems to deny that this is so and that improvement in usage appears to be more effectively achieved through practice of desirable forms than through memorisation of rules.

Wilkinson (1964) reviews a number of experimental studies which indicate that learning grammar has no beneficial effect on children. This conclusion is supported by the work of Harris (1962, 1965) who studied progress in writing skills in five matched pairs of forms over a two-year period among children aged twelve to fourteen. In each pair one form had a weekly lesson on English grammar, while the other had further practice in writing. The work was assessed on a number of objective measures of structural skills at the beginning and end of the two-year period. The grammar lesson was found in most cases inferior to direct practice in writing.

If children are given the opportunity to write freely, they will demonstrate the errors in punctuation and spelling which they need help to overcome. On many occasions group errors will occur which justify formal lessons to correct common faults, but more often correction can be individual, and so timed that it will in no way reduce the child's spontaneity in his writing. Fluency must not be discouraged at the expense of correction.

The setting up of an effective environment for creative writing is a highly individual matter in which a friendly relationship between teacher and pupil is very important. Evaluation, therefore, must be carefully considered. It is very difficult to evaluate a creative product and the approach will vary according to school, class, and teacher. The activity is more important than the end-product, but that must, of necessity, be given serious consideration. Quality is important and must be assessed if any improvement is to be made. Attention must be given to the content of the work, the thought which produced it, and the effort made. Gradually the child must be made to feel that his work is an extension of himself. He should therefore not fear the consequences of genuine failure and yet should understand that he must never deliberately misuse his time and material.

Rigid lesson plans which expect a display at the end of every lesson are of little value, but since the essential purpose of any creative work is communication with others, it is necessary for children who wish to share their work with others to have the opportunity of doing so. Often a display of work stimulates pupils to strive for a high standard of execution and, in the right circumstances, children displaying their work have an opportunity to discuss and to experiment with their skills.

At the *infant school* level talking, reading and writing are interdependent, all being relevant to the total experience of the child. As fluency and reading develop, children desire to describe their individual experiences with hardly any thought of the difficulties of expression. They will also wish to relate imaginary or 'let's pretend' stories, often helping themselves in finding words from lists or from the ever-willing teacher. The stimulus of experience both at first-hand and indirectly through lessons and books will develop a sensitivity for words. Activities for infants involve recording experiences of significance to them, drawing and writing about pictures or stories (made-up or retold). Much of this work can take place in a 'writing corner'.

A teacher after a talk on the senses to a class of six-year-olds received these interesting descriptions.

'The silk is smooth to touch. It makes a sound like grease frying.'
'Fur feels like an old mat.'

'The orange paper is crunchie it sounds like wind in the trees.'
'Silk is soft and nice. It makes a noise like crisps.'
'The sweet paper makes a noise like a crackling fire.'
'Sponges are ruff but not bad pillows.'
'Coal is shiny, black and cold and hot later.'
'The putty of dough, the heart of bread.'
'A veil is like wire-netting on your face.'

While it must be realised that the translation of feelings and thoughts into words is a difficult process for a young child, and that writing is even more difficult since emphasis and intonation must somehow be communicated, by the last year in the infant school some approximation to the conventions of spelling and punctuation becomes necessary. If encouraged to read what they have written, children may see the purpose behind simple punctuation. Correction should be individual and always in the presence of the child.

When children transfer to the *junior school* or section, fluency must not be endangered by over-emphasis on formal exercises and neatness. As in the infant school, it is essential to have a reason for writing, and time and opportunity for doing so. There is a close connection between speech, writing and all the other activities of junior school work—environmental studies, mathematics, science, and other areas of study—indeed, all those occasions when children need to record or communicate their thoughts. It is hardly necessary to list writing separately because it should permeate nearly all the programme. Junior children delight in playing with words, searching for those which give exactly the shade of meaning they wish to convey, and they sometimes have pleasure in creating words to do this. Abundant practice in metaphor, simile and word-coinages is not only creative in itself but a necessary preparation for the development of creative expression.

A teacher read the opening speech from Dylan Thomas's *Under Milk Wood* to a class of ten-year-olds, and then asked the children to describe their own house and town in the middle of the night. This description by Pauline was one of a number of interesting pieces of writing.

Dark town, sleeping, snoring, dreaming town, resting town. Old, ancient, crumbled buildings, inhabited only by mice. Glittering, star studded, tar black sky, sleeping sky. Moonlight night, heavenly night. The waves resting on the soft sea, the soft, fishy tranquil sea. Shoes, small shoes, big shoes, scattered all around. Not a sound. New cars, old cars at the sides of the streets, the dusty dirty, humanless streets. Dentures resting in their watery beds, resting at their owners' sides. Faithful teeth, clean, white, hard working teeth, but some dirty. Warm, cosy, cushy, soft beds and pillowy feathery pillows, resting pillows. Resting kitchen, empty of Mother. Pots, pans laying waiting, sleeping crockery, all ready for morning.

One medium of creative expression suitable for all three stages of schooling is verse-writing. Children love poetry and enjoy sounds, unusual combinations of words, a sense of rhyme and rhythm, although rhyming patterns can sometimes hamper rather than encourage the creative process. Children must never be made to feel that they have to find a word that rhymes, for this can inhibit natural expression. Their spontaneous language is often poetic in nature. Because of this children do not find writing verse more difficult than writing prose if they are given suitable guidance.

In the early stages they should not be expected to adhere to balanced rhyme and metre. What can be achieved very early is simple arrangement of lines and a rhythmical speech pattern. Topics may have to be suggested, and observation stimulated by discussion. The reading of well-selected poems, by both teachers and children, will help to convey the idea that poetic expression is precise, economic, and emotional. Early exercises will concentrate on elementary aspects of technique, words that make sounds and convey pictures, and planned repetition of words and phrases. Later, useful complementary exercises might include rhyming patterns, alliteration, similes and metaphors.

Satisfying and imaginative poems should be read out, and possibly recorded in the form of individual, class, or school anthologies, which might be illustrated.

The aim of verse-writing will not be to produce a class of poets, but to allow to every individual child the satisfaction of expressing his thoughts and feelings succinctly and with precision.

In the *secondary school* young pupils are very interested in emotional experience and will frequently express their feelings in writing before they discuss them freely with adults. Writing is a way in which they explore their own minds and come to terms with their thoughts. Developing creative writing at this stage involves emotional sensitivity and training in accurate observation. Language, which hitherto had been a vehicle of communication with other people, now becomes also the means by which the pupil can advance his own thoughts and feelings.

The wise teacher will help his pupils to realise that a considerable variety of ideas can be ordered into various patterns by selection and organisation. Experiment will be coupled with discipline so that the child enjoys that sense of fulfilment which every craftsman enjoys. Techniques, even at this stage, should whenever possible be taught not in isolation but in relation to significant individual ideas. Personally-motivated learning is always better than a formal set exercise, and young people should be encouraged rather than driven to write.

This piece of writing by Joan (aged 14), who had a free choice of topic, gives an insight into the development of an adolescent's personality. Her main interests are apparent—dress, figure, boyfriends, and the adult world which she will soon be entering. She also expresses her frustration with what seems to her an inappropriate curriculum and at the considerable inequality and suffering she recognises around her.

> The young girl sat looking around her. She was the slimmest girl in the examination room, but obviously not the most educated because everyone else was writing like mad. Her mind strayed to the Youth Club Dance last Friday where her green mini-dress with white trimmings had been admired by everyone, to the Discotheque last night where she had worn her blue bell-bottoms and frilly blouse and had been picked up by the most handsome boy there. Suddenly she was jerked from her reverie by the tweedy voice of Miss Hawk saying, "Only half an hour to go." She brushed her pony-tail back over her head and worked in earnest—for five minutes! It was no use. "Roll on next year when I leave," she said. "How does all this help the poor, the old and the sick anyway? How does it help me? Roll on."

Joan had spent all her secondary school life in a non-academic stream, but Rachel (age 12), a grammar school pupil, had enjoyed writing creatively for some time. In this extract from a piece called 'Neptune's Paradise' one can sense her enjoyment at writing adventurously and her aesthetic delight at combining words.

The coral they had stopped at was coloured in shades of pearly pinks and pale blues and yellows.
Sea anemones moaned quietly on the rocks' sides, waiting for one of the small fish to fall into its clutches. A thing so beautiful and yet so dangerous to the fish.
The flowers were clustered together in one huge mass of riotous colour—rippling with the rhythmic motion of the sea.

At all stages the school's aim must be to obtain from children pieces of writing which they have been inspired to write and which they have enjoyed. The teacher needs to provide the fresh and challenging opportunities and experiences, the materials and the stimulation needed, and discreetly and tactfully teach the necessary skills at the appropriate stage of development. Creative expression will develop harmoniously with an ever-improving standard of execution as the children mature, and the child's own work can be made the basis of instruction aimed at refining expression and improving accuracy.

Art and Craft

The urge to create something beautiful is a very basic one, and should this lead a child to express himself graphically, rather than through words or music, he may try his skill in painting, drawing, or sculpture. In the past art and craft have often been relegated to a minor place in the curricula of the schools because, it was claimed, they had little direct contribution to vocational academic and social achievement. They were often considered only in the light of their usefulness to other subjects, such as history, geography, social studies, or mathematics. But art and craft exist in their own right as important sources of creative experience. They provide the child with opportunities to explore and express feelings about himself and the world around him, they strengthen his abilities to observe, to imagine and to feel; and if he is permitted a degree of choice in his work and materials, he will gain a sense of responsibility, judgment and control. They also supply an opportunity to express feelings and experiences which the child would find difficult to express in words. They may have therapeutic value by relieving tension, or may simply provide pleasurable experiences in re-living absorbing experiences or rearranging these in new combinations and satisfying ways.

If the teacher is going to succeed in guiding his pupils to satisfying creative expression in the art and craft programme, he will have to create an atmosphere in which this is possible. He will believe that each child possesses, to some degree, artistic qualities; he will ensure that his pupils gain frequent success-experiences in order to establish a worthy self-concept, and he will come to accept the unpredictable which the child offers. He will respect the child's individuality by increasingly giving him a measure of choice and responsibility in his work. He will provide verbal stimulation where necessary, but will deliberately refrain from solving problems for the child. He will realise that artistic and constructive creativity is a slow, gradual process, requiring patience from both teacher and pupil. He will recognise, also, the subtle and important part played by evaluation, so that creative expression can not only flower but flourish and progress.

In the *infant school* the child will take the first definite and formative steps towards creative expression, and foundations will be laid in artistic and constructive work. Children of this age are capable of producing exciting and uninhibited work, but can be so influenced by parents and teachers that they lose their unselfconscious and free style and produce not what they like, but what they think grown-ups will like.

The teacher must provide conditions for imaginative and artistic development. At best, creative expression will be stimulated and a set of skills acquired for later work; at worst, the work will be equated with a limited range of imitative responses in which every child conforms to a set pattern. The pupils can be restricted by the teacher's attitude, by a rigid adherance to the setting of class topics, and by the amount and nature of the materials provided for their use.

A great variety of materials should be available to intrigue the child and catch his attention. Large quantities are required of different kinds of paper, card, paints, crayons, chalks, charcoal, wood, clay, and such other materials as can easily be acquired by the children: feathers, corks, scraps of cloth, matchboxes, cottonreels, and indeed almost any object. There must be freedom and time to explore these materials, and young children will learn a great deal simply by selecting and comparing them. This encounter with a variety of materials should take place throughout the child's schooling, and even at the infants' level evidence of any individual style should be looked for and welcomed.

The teacher creates an atmosphere of freedom in which children can move and explore with very little restriction. But very soon they must understand that freedom has limits and carries responsibilities. One individual's creative growth should not be achieved at the expense of that of his peers.

Allowance should be made for the short attention-span of young children by offering them a choice of several activities. When the basic skills of holding a brush, mixing colour, and cutting card have been mastered, a measure of freedom and choice can be given. Evaluation at this stage must be avoided if it is likely to lead to a loss of self-confidence. There are no clear-cut standards which teachers can use in interpreting the significance of the young child's creative work with regard to content, colours, or organisation. Sometimes the content of the drawings, paintings and models is a direct statement of the child's feelings, but more often it is a symbolic statement related to ideas or pre-occupations, and the significance of each symbol varies from child to child. Teachers should not try to read a great deal into a single piece of creative work, or ask the child to explain his thoughts and feelings unless the child obviously wishes to discuss his work. The satisfaction the child experiences in the creative process is more important than the evaluation of the resulting product.

Nevertheless, infants require guidance and suggestion if their attempts to express ideas and feelings through creative channels are to succeed. Too much freedom will often lead to repetitive and unimaginative work. Help must be given when the child is evidently frustrated because he is not able to express himself. While imagination and spontaneity are vital, it is the teacher's duty to 'open doors for the children to enter which otherwise would forever remain closed to them'.

As well as creating the appropriate classroom atmosphere, providing a variety of materials and tactful guidance, infant school teachers must endeavour to act as interpreters of the art and craft-work of children to their parents. The occasions when parents meet teachers are opportunities for them to become acquainted with the artistic qualities displayed by children and the developmental stages through which they pass. The restrictive nature of many colouring books can be pointed out, and suitable materials and conditions suggested by means of which children can enjoy creative work at home.

It is natural for all children to pass through stages in their art and craft-work, although the rate at which they do so varies considerably and does not fall conveniently into infant, junior and secondary. When a child's work indicates that he has entered a new stage of development, he has enlarged his self-concept and is committing himself to the new stage in his created product.

In the *junior school* there is sometimes a decline in the quality of art and craft work compared with that done in the infants' school. This is attributed to a more formal approach, more imitative work, a demand for greater skill, and less scope for the child's personal involvement. There must be a correct balance between free expression and the development of technique. Already the child may show preference for one media or kind of work over another. He should be encouraged in this preference, but also be given the experience of different kinds of work and material. In addition to giving plenty of visual stimulation and free expression, the teacher should help the child to a knowledge of techniques he is unlikely to discover unaided. This must be regarded as an important means to an even more important end— the development of creative expression. Techniques learned in early childhood, simple though they may be, form the basis of later development. Teachers must not expect children to be able to operate new materials and techniques successfully during early encounters with them. The pleasure of discovery for the child with access to a variety of materials will add significance to his work and ultimately enable him to enjoy a wide range of creative experience. For example, the delight of children in experimenting with new colour combinations helps them to express feelings and ideas which are developing gradually in subtlety.

After new techniques have been mastered, creativity should be encouraged and imitation and copying discouraged. The work should be based on understanding and the acceptance of personal and aesthetic growth. Progress can be ensured by encouraging a better standard of finish, by handling more challenging materials and stimulating more challenging topics in the same media.

Plastic, expanded polystyrene and self-fixing dyes, and easily accessible non-art material of all kinds, broadens the children's awareness of the expressive potential of mundane material. A picture no longer consists only of oil paint, pastels, or water-colours, and sculpture traditionally made of stone or bronze is now composed of anything and everything and is simply an art form in three dimensions. D. Z. Meilach's *Creating Art from*

Anything (Pitman, 1971) offers excellent examples of work in a very wide variety of materials. The work will, at this stage, include new media and procedures, and the reinforcement of familiar one-, two- and three-dimensional work, variety in size, and in group and individual activity. In the last two years of the junior school, particularly, children can be introduced to pottery, woodcarving, lino-cutting and fabric printing, and even simple screen printing. In painting and drawing, water-colour or poster-paint can be combined with crayon or pastel, and there should be frequent experiment in colour and texture. The composition of the picture must be considered and its dependence upon varied arrangement of line, shape and tone understood. Needlecraft, embroidery and weaving should now be developed as arts, not merely as skills, and the embroidered or woven picture, garment, or article for the home can combine usefulness and creative expression.

Junior children are still not ready for an analytical approach to their creative work. They must be allowed to lose themselves in their work and to enjoy it with sincerity of thought and feeling. There must be a feeling of progress, however, and a quiet insistence on good finish and the best technique of which the child is capable.

By the time the children have reached the *secondary stage* they have progressed mentally from exploring the properties of materials to using them in making their own clear and detailed communication. Their intellectual development is at an advanced stage of growth, and many of them can now invent new ways of using materials and can refine methods previously used. As they are better able to define problems and seek solutions, so they grow in creative ability. This will be successfully expressed if they are given the teacher's approval and interest, suitable materials and working conditions, and expert guidance when they ask for it.

A teacher who welcomes ideas, and creates an atmosphere in which the pupils are challenged by their own perceptions, will give children confidence in their ability to communicate and to establish their own style in doing so. On giving form to his vision, the pupil accepts responsibility for what he creates. He will often need periods of apparently slow activity to assemble resources, and the shrewd teacher will distinguish between necessary mental preparation and laziness.

Pictures may be based upon groups of displayed objects, or

may be imaginary or abstract. In paintings, drawings, patterns and designs there cannot be progressive subject matter suitable to all the children. Work at this stage can show more specialisation. There is room to introduce heavy, light and domestic crafts, and a large number of challenging activities such as sculpture in wood, clay or even nails, carving in plaster, salt, wood and sandstone, decorated pottery, candle-making, original and experimental embroidery, all kinds of basketry and weaving, textile printing, and mosaic work in a number of media. These activities will result in creative work only if there is at least enjoyment in exercising different techniques, if the products bear the mark of the creator's individual style, thought and feeling, if the child has established his identity through his work. At this advanced stage the pupil initiates and carries out work which he sets himself and the resulting product bears the mark of his personal quality and individuality.

Creative work in the arts and crafts can be described as a continuing search for order and harmony and as an attempt to resolve problems of one's relationship to the environment. This view helps to reduce present divisions between subjects, and sees art and craft as links between many areas of the curriculum.

After the child has expressed himself through drawing, painting, or modelling, he is often able to verbalise more freely. Painting a picture stimulated by historical studies enables him to experience a living encounter with the past. Work in science can contribute in its demand for attention to detail of shapes and forms in the environment, and implications for mathematics, geography and most of the other traditional disciplines become apparent.

If art and craft are taught creatively, they will enable the child to come to terms with deep feelings and emotions which are of fundamental importance to personal development. If the child is guided to a discovery that he has something to say and the means with which to express it, he will communicate with confidence and sensitivity, he will experience the harmony that comes with individual and constructive action, and grow in sensitive appreciation of the visual arts, of design, of the environment, and of the universe.

Expressive and Dramatic Movement

Children have a natural desire for movement. As they proceed from the nursery school to the middle and upper stages of their schooling, their play drive must be harnessed. Not only is the whole range of play displayed in body movement, but there exists a pleasure of mastery in repetition, and in the expression of emotions and experience. If children are to be physically adequate, creative, imaginative, and expressive in movement, the school must provide planned educational experience, usually through physical education, which centres in movement and develops physical skill, power, and pleasure.

Intellectual, physical and emotional development have their roots in action and exploration through the senses and through movement, but children need more than activity. They need to obtain a feeling of self-mastery, and require freedom to choose different movements and to perform these in a variety of ways in working out their ideas. The old drill and physical training programmes of years ago consisted of formal exercises involving very little imagination and choice. Programmes which followed were based on the Swedish system and devoted much care to exercise of the whole body in a variety of ways. Modern programmes explore and extend physical powers, prepare children for corporate living, and attempt to develop reflective and creative thinking.

In the past most movements were performed by command and in unison, the pace invariably being set by the teachers. But exploration and creativity take *time*, because new movements and ideas cannot be worked out unless a considerable portion of time is allotted to experimentation.

Modern movement lessons emphasise the development of the child as an individual. Motivation is supplied by apparatus, natural obstacles, game-like activities and tasks set by the teacher. Functional work—running, leaping, climbing and swinging—develop confidence, poise, mobility and strength, and are a necessary complement to expressive work. Once basic skills of movement are mastered, variations in the factors of space, time, and weight follow. Progression can take place in many ways, since movements can form sequences and patterns, either individually or in groups. The teachers guide their pupils by challenges so that 'movement-answers' can be produced within the limits of their ability and the space provided. Worth-while movement solutions require thought from both teachers and pupils, so that challenges advance in complexity and require increasing physical and mental effort. To arrange the time and opportunity for individual movement does not mean that the teacher confines himself to a purely passive role. The process of learning proceeds with an exchange of ideas, arising from carefully planned stituations. If the teacher can evoke development rather than command it, the child's movement experience will be enriched, and opportunities will be provided for effective and satisfying work far beyond the demands made by the performance of a limited range of exercises and agilities, which will provide a pool from which creative skill in dance and drama can be developed.

A new conception of expressive movement based on the exploitation of various aspects and qualities of body movement leading to dramatic expression is associated with the name of Rudolf Laban. He pioneered the idea that the body should be regarded as a medium for the communication of ideas and feelings, and that each person possesses specific movement characteristics. The teacher must be ready to give technical advice without ever impairing the enjoyment of the children, and must suggest suitable themes, giving constant stimulation to further inventiveness, demanding increasing mental effort and concentration. Eventually the child realises that a certain amount of discipline, skill and technique is needed for self-satisfaction.

Creative dance can be defined as the spontaneous re-enactment of emotion in movement. The dance, in school work, utilizes movements to express ideas, thoughts and actions, sometimes unaccompanied, but often stimulated by music, percussion, stories, or poems. This type of work demands both personal and group involvement in which children explore the limitations and potential of their own bodies and minds. Feeling and thought are expressed through movement, which for very young children is more expressive than speech. Through movement and dance, many children are enabled to explore areas of experience which may not yet be accessible to them through words.

In the *infants' school* themes involving both movement and stillness must be carefully chosen to excite and stimulate, yet should not suggest that dancing is only for girls and the genteel and effeminate boy. There should be very little imitation of

c

others' movements, and the teacher's voice is an important means of inspiration. Since infants will find difficulty in understanding abstract terminology, simple movement words, such as 'gallop', 'leap' and 'grow', must be used. *Juniors* can build up a vocabulary of movement terms. Stories, suggested by the children themselves, can stimulate the imagination. More use can be made of interplay between groups, but there should be considerable individuality within them. If in the primary school child there has developed a movement awareness, namely of body, space and effort, a firm foundation has been laid for creative dance in the *secondary school*. A more abstract terminology can now be understood and deep group feeling developed. Dance studies, group dances, and dance dramas requiring more teacher direction can now effectively take place.

Dramatic expression emerges from dance and movement. Again the creative process will be initiated by the teacher, but will take place within the individual. Drama is emotional and a form of acting out emotional situations has been called 'psycho-drama' and used in adult therapy. The values of this for children cannot be overestimated, because not only is there a therapeutic factor at work, but by acting out their inhibitions they come to understand the properties and significance of movement and how these are related to situation and character. Experience is acted out by children as they are guided in thinking, feeling and creating their own dialogue and action. In the early stages, no lines should be memorised and no formal audience or technical aids considered. Dramatisation may be original, or based on a poem or story written by someone else. The two essentials are space in which to move, and ideas from which to create movement and mime or dialogue. The general progression seems to be creative play in the infants' department, improvisation in the junior section, polished improvisation in the lower secondary level and, in addition to all these, complete plays for the upper secondary children.

The teacher's part throughout these stages should be carefully considered. Peter Slade (1954) stressed the importance of 'In-flow' (a taking in of ideas) and 'Out-flow' (a pouring out of creative forms of expression) which with exercise can result in and promote confidence in this type of work. This approach seems to be based on sound common sense because it combines a reasonable scope for free expression and a developing discipline.

The teacher must not allow any one child to persist in behaviour which interferes gravely with the freedom of others. He must ensure that progression takes place, and yet he must give abundant scope for the individual expression of every child. He must not be tempted in the early stages to produce formal plays for the appreciation of audiences because his aim is to develop the expression of feeling rather than skilled and formal gestures. He must beware of misusing any situation for adult purposes. Undue competitive performance may create tension and over-stimulation, to the detriment of an informal and spontaneous atmosphere. The teacher's task is to offer to children exciting situations which stimulate their own movement and language flow, so that they can explore their emotions and feelings and later control them sensitively. What is needed is the expression of the personality of the child and not an impression of the personality of the teacher.

In the *infants' section*, play is all important. Children at this stage wish to express themselves through action. Rhythmic movement, sounds, songs, finger plays, nursery rhymes, and stories will all stimulate expressive action. Properties should be used sparingly, audiences hardly at all, and costumes only if there can be a creative selection of odds and ends. The teacher must not spend too long in talking and planning, because infants are eager to do, to act, and to play a role. When children are thinking and feeling and sensing in character, their actions and speech will be spontaneous. There is an important difference between playing a role and memorising lines written by someone else.

The experienced and perceptive teacher will come to know when to offer suggestions for improving technique and for stimulation. In general, the right moment will be when the children's own invention is no longer enough to satisfy them. When spontaneity flags, guidance is needed.

In the *junior section*, too, there must not be too much interference with creative expression, and for most of the time the teacher must confine himself to helping with ideas and organisation of materials, time and space. Discussion should be short and formal techniques generally avoided. Much use can be made of mime and movement in dramatic work, and puppetry and sound-effects work can be introduced when appropriate. Some formal play-acting can take place in the upper junior school, particularly if there is room for modification of written plays to suit the children and to accommodate every member of the class.

At this stage there should be opportunity for simple, original play-writing by the children, both individually and in groups. All these forms used in primary dramatic work can be utilised and extended at *secondary school* level, and at no time should the creative and spontaneous approach be abandoned. But there is now room also for planned, memorised and directed plays. A successful performance, involving some instruction in proscenium, rostrum, lighting and staging techniques, can make dramatic activity more meaningful and delightful than ever before. The children must be guided to understand that play-writing and play-singing and play-acting are all highly creative actions involving individual choice and expression.

At this level, too, much use can be made of simple socio-drama, a discussion method combined with drama. The procedure usually is for a group to observe a few of its fellow-members playing out a situation based on real or imaginary situations—family, social, or occupational. Activity concerned with this form of communication demands a relaxed and uncritical receiving situation and, because discussion and acting follow each other spontaneously, the method gives a measure of both emotional involvement and therapeutic release.

At all stages of schooling it is highly desirable that there should be a close connection between dramatic and other time-table subjects. Dramatic work is most useful in stimulating hand-work and art in the creation of 'props', costumes, simple scenery, masks, posters, and notices; in creative writing in accounts of plays and play composition; in physical education in stimulating expressive movement (which must at no stage be disconnected from dramatic work). Indeed, most of the conventional subjects in the school programme can have a close affinity with dramatic work.

A thoughtful programme of expressive and dramatic move-ment put into operation will produce creative thinking and acting individuals, for such work is not so much 'doing' as 'being', the very essence of life itself.

Science

Science and mathematics are very closely related. Both involve similar mental processes, personal experience, observation, ex-ploration and critical thinking. Yet despite their close connection, both disciplines have specific aspects which require a separate approach.

Science makes observations, designs and performs controlled experiments, asks questions, formulates hypotheses and draws conclusions. Traditional school science strongly emphasised the acquisition of knowledge through the analysis of facts and figures. It was regarded as a body of facts to be accepted rather than as a method of investigation. Although the best teachers always appealed to their pupils' sense of wonder, much of the work in schools degenerated into a morass of isolated facts. What was not given prominence was the creative use of knowledge.

The teaching of science has undergone a radical change over the last twenty years. The best work is now directed towards a true understanding of how man can know and improve his environment. The emphasis is on the scientific process practised individually by children involving a significant proportion of problem-solving situations. The admission of a 'dignity of doubt' has moved the onus from the teacher to the pupil, and, not knowing what the outcome of an experiment will be, the child is very much in the role of the researcher—the professional scientist. In working out and setting scientific problems for themselves, children have to think independently in challenging situations. In observing facts, designing experiments, classifying them, perceiving relationships, drawing conclusions, and then recording his discoveries, the pupil is working in a highly creative way with a sense of pleasure and purpose.

Although the teacher has to provide materials, create challenging situations and overcome initial difficulties through questioning and suggesting, he must not give so much help that responsibility and initiative are removed from the child. Syllabuses must be sufficiently flexible to allow the children to follow their own line of interest and yet be sufficiently comprehensive to ensure a reasonable coverage of the fields of science and give an appropriate balance between planned and unplanned activities. Attitudes of mind and ways of learning are more important than the acquisition of facts.

Sophistication of treatment, choice of topics and relative emphasis will differ markedly at each level of schooling, even though the general objectives are the same. The Nuffield Science Schemes (the Junior Science Scheme designed for children from five to thirteen, and Secondary Science for ages thirteen to sixteen, and the O- and A-level Schemes) transcend conventional traditional organisation divisions and are based on close observation of children of different levels and their responses to scientific situations.

In the *infants' school* the child is observed in taking in new experiences, finding names for them, and organising these into new patterns. Because first-hand practical experience is the key to understanding, the first necessity is for the schools to organise situations and supply materials which children would explore and examine for themselves. It is not enough to take children out to discover their environment, or to leave them to their own devices. Significant, too, is the discussion which takes place between teacher and child because this is the way in which new words, attitudes and judgments are consolidated. The child's questions must be answered with kindness and enthusiasm because these are the key to continuing motivation and future progress.

The child needs time to play about in order to come to terms with experiences and materials—for example, to dabble with water if he is later to understand its properties. He must be given opportunities to compare, classify, investigate, observe, describe, and to share his findings and feelings with his peers and his teacher.

The old nature table may well have made way for the science corner in which pets are kept, books and materials are displayed, opportunities for experiment can take place, and there is room for the child's expressive work resulting from his observations and his growing experience.

In the *junior school* children may be observed experimenting and recording at a more advanced level. They will experiment with water, pulleys, Meccano, jars of insects; they will preserve tracks in plaster casts, keep tape recordings as a form of electronic notebook. The principle of continuity is preserved by means of the natural order, and pupils will observe changes in plants, stars, and the habits of animals according to the changing seasons. In addition, they can be introduced to simple principles of magnetism, electricity, mechanics, heat, sound and light.

They will increasingly desire to express their findings in writing, in number, and by pictures and diagrams. They will need to communicate not only in materials but also in words. Discussion sharpens interest and builds up a vocabulary which must constantly expand.

Whilst predetermined lines of enquiry are not in line with the child's growing independence (which is why some science kits and stereotyped assignment cards must be regarded with caution), if he is left completely to himself to experiment with materials and nature around him he will reach only a limited level of scientific development. Individual child-investigation may lead to exciting discoveries, but situations must be *planned* in order to ensure maximum opportunity for learning.

At junior level, too, there must be close integration with work in almost every other area of the curriculum. Very effective writing can be evoked by the upper junior child's close involvement in his activity and the resulting desire to communicate a personal experience. Creative expression can take place also in diagrammatic, pictorial, and display work as well as in the more subtle approaches involving discovery and problem solving. Interesting research work on the formation of the scientific concepts of children between the ages of eight and twelve with particular reference to teaching method has been taking place at the Univerisity College of North Wales, Bangor. This and similar research will eventually facilitate the creative potential of scientific work in the schools.

At the *secondary level* the central theme is still the environmental and physical control of living things. Hitherto division within the sciences, physical and biological, would have been artificial. Now because of the child's increasing need for knowledge and his mental development this division becomes not only desirable but necessary. There must still be room, however, for extensive individual pupil-experiment. Experience in primary science is not only valuable in itself, but makes children readier to deal with the more systematic approach in the secondary school.

The course at this level should still focus on the nature of scientific inquiry, but also present substantial bodies of modern knowledge and concepts. A coherent picture should be presented of biology, chemistry and physics and the logical interconnection of these disciplines as well as the social implications of science. At present attempts are being made at the sixth-form stage to integrate concepts in physics and chemistry by approaching the physical sciences, for example, by means of the electron, the atom, the wave, and the study of energy.

It needs to be emphasised that division of science into its separate disciplines does not, to any extent, exclude creative thinking and work. The study of biology, for example, should be presented always as a living subject and not as a catalogue of terms to be memorised. Even at sixth-form level, when the biological sciences are usually divided into botany and zoology, students should learn by their own observations. Chemistry, the study of matter and its interactions, is broadened out to include the qualitative nature of chemical composition and reaction. The teacher may limit the materials and the reaction variables chosen for study, thus opening up an important field for exploration and discovery. In physics, subject matter should include studies of the atom, the electron, kinetic theory, and a breadth of other phenomena. Apparatus can be carefully designed so that discovery involves a thoughtful contribution from the pupil. Domestic science, now more appropriately called home economics, consists of the study of those arts and applied sociological sciences relevant to home-making and home management. A creative approach can be introduced in the preparation of nutritious and attractive foods, and in discussion and planning of interior decoration, where design and choice of materials, equipment and furniture is a personal and individual venture.

At primary and secondary levels, it is vital to emphasise that science has an important aesthetic aspect. There is beauty not only in nature, in the snowflake, the flower, the animal, and the crystal, but also in the pattern, the spatial, quantitative and measurable aspects which become evident in the analysis of nature. A creative approach to science helps the child to understand and come to terms with the world around him, and the creative expression of this understanding is given a more precise dimension.

Mathematics

If we are to believe with Galileo that mathematics is the language in which God has written the Universe, we must realise that it has both an utilitarian and cultural element. The language of mathematics communicates the structure of the world, its order and pattern. It provides aesthetic appeal not only in the form displayed by environment, but also in the satisfaction of discovering solutions and perceiving similarities.

Over the last twenty years there has been a decisive change in the teaching of mathematics. The old method was usually rote-learning which developed computational skill without logical reasoning. Children were taught how to manipulate numbers long before they understood their underlying structure. Computational accuracy is still the core of mathematical teaching, but today children are presented with familiar situations, and taught to regard mathematics as stages of discovery which foster a critical and creative as well as a logical turn of mind. Much emphasis is placed on acquiring mathematical experience by guided exploration of structured apparatus. The systems devised by Dienes, Stern, and Cuisenaire have been the most popular. In these approaches, children are encouraged to formulate rules and methods of computation for themselves, and indeed are stimulated to be creative. The best results occur when the introduction of new content (simple statistics, scale of notation, geometry, sets) has been combined with a move towards individualised learning (see *Mathematics in Primary Schools: Schools Council Curriculum Bulletin No. 1*).

Over the years observations, particularly of Jean Piaget, have led to new thoughts on the ways in which children learn, and the ages and stages at which they are ready to acquire various concepts. This has led to the view of mathematics as a developing structure of ideas logically related.

This process is immediately in evidence at the *infants'* stage, when progress depends on personal factors, on inherent ability and early experience. Each child is guided to progress according to his own rate and developmental pattern as he acquires number vocabulary and elementary computational skill based on understanding in a functional setting. He gradually develops independence in understanding and skills as he attacks new problems.

No formal period of mathematics is advisable in the early stages, but experiences and activities can be planned so that teaching is developed through *incidental* and not *accidental* experiences. Situations will be created, and others will arise spontaneously, out of which mathematical ideas will appear. Concepts of equality and of contrasting sizes and shapes are introduced and used informally, but provisions for these activities are often planned consciously by the teacher.

One important activity is playing with shapes and sorting them into labelled groups. Some chocolate boxes are useful to show triangular prisms, bottles and tins to show cylinders, egg-boxes to show irregular shapes, and ice-cream cornets to show cones. Later this work will progress to discover, for example, that triangles can strengthen buildings, that cranes (real and Meccano) are full of triangles, that a cylinder is an economic shape to package liquid in, and that many right angled, circular, and diagonal shapes are found in nature. Work in infant schools has shown three fundamental changes for the better. First, there has been a change in the teaching of computation in which the fundaments and structure of the number processes have been emphasised, while meaningless memory exercises have been generally discarded. Number situations arise from real situations in the child's environment. Six- and seven-year-olds enjoy measuring and weighing out ingredients, and carefully take cognisance of the time needed for cooking. Work is often extended to include number bases, sets, and as an extension of numbers to include integers and rationals. Secondly, infant teachers have taken a broader look at geometric ideas, and shapes and symmetry have become an important part of infant school activities. Thirdly, there has been a much wider application of pictorial and graphical representation. Graphs of numbers of things, from milk-bottles to socks, from birthdays to National Savings, have appeared and the children frequently match, relate and classify objects and numbers.

The infant teacher's work can be summarised as the provision of materials and situations for creative, imaginative and imitative play which offer children a purposeful approach to a wider mathematical background.

By the beginning of the *junior school* stage the child should be maturing confidently in his ability to reason ways in which to solve problems intelligently and creatively. In the past at this level the mathematical education of most children was too exclusively restricted to computation, but if the creative approach progresses from the infant school, much stimulating work can be achieved.

At some stage in the junior school the children must be expected to learn, systematically (but not laboriously), addition, subtraction, multiplication and division facts. Progress in creative work is slow until these are known, but once these facts are automatic energies are left free for more advanced thought. Mathematics can be closely linked with language, environmental studies, art and craft, and science, and representational and graphical work of all kinds becomes possible. Upper juniors experience real mathematical insight while studying number and space. They can discover the excitement and understanding of concepts, having moved from play to experiment, and from experiment to regular patterns underlying experience.

The next stage is that of logical development, the checking, the proving and the starting of the finished form. But to over-stress this stage is to rob mathematics of much of its excitement and most of its creative element. Exploration, discovery, arrangement and choice should receive full encouragement also in the *secondary school* curriculum, which should be continuous with the new primary school approach, enlarging and enriching the concepts already acquired.

Full appreciation of the power and generality of mathematics as an abstract logical science is only possible in late adolescence. At this stage the average child is capable of reversible formal operations and can deduce conclusions from abstract hypotheses. Subject matter may be developed more systematically, but should continue to arise from real situations. Sets and logic, function, algebra, geometry, number systems, simple statistics, and trigonometry can all be given attention, and advanced principles of mechanics and motions of the heavenly bodies explained mathematically.

Mathematics, taught progressively, leads to orderly sensible thinking and organisation of experience—all prerequisites of the creative process. This is because in all mathematical work, from the elementary to the advanced, is inherent a measure of elegance, pattern, and order.

Music

Music is a significant element of the culture which it is the re-sponsibility of the school to transmit, and musical experiences are an integral part of many activities of learning, providing a valuable contribution to the development of each child according to his invididual pattern of growth and development.

The school's aim is not to produce trained musicians, but to develop an awareness, sensitivity, understanding, basic knowledge of and pleasure in music. In particular, music is a creative activity because it leads to exploration and personal experience. A good school musical programme offers opportunities for listening, singing, and creating, involving rhythmic responses and the play-ing of instruments individually and in groups.

Traditionally many of the school musical activities were

concerned with singing, with interpreting and reproducing sounds, and with techniques. The important element missing was exploration and individual first-hand experience.

Creative work of this kind is associated with the name of Carl Orff who suggests the use of the pentatonic scale at an early age to avoid unnecessary difficulties. Orff showed how verbal rhythms could be explored by using children's names and those of plants and animals. From this, quite complex effects can be built up. For example, the duple rhythm of 'Donald' can develop to the triplet rhythm of 'daffodil'. Step by step children are enabled to transfer the same rhythms to tuned percussion instruments, working out patterns for themselves, and making up their own accompaniments without having to worry whether these will fit in harmoniously. Individual work can be supplemented by group-work involving team patterns, and at a later stage children can work on the rhythm of nursery rhymes, bringing out their interpretation of words. This approach exploits the close relationship between language and musical rhythm and provides situations in which children can explore, improvise and create music. Even here there must be selection, control and technique if work is to progress, and teachers can use Orff principles according to their own teaching situations.

It must be emphasised that the Orff approach is not the only creative one in music. Some critics of Orff-*Schulwerk* have claimed that in this approach there is no guarantee of aural perception, an important aim of all music teaching, because insufficient use is made of the human voice and eventually too much of instruments. The Kodaly method avoids the use of instruments and concentrates entirely on vocal exercises beginning with a pentatonic framework, the use of hand signs, and the encouragement of vocal improvisation. The less publicised method of George Self has a number of enthusiastic supporters. This approach attempts to solve the problem of structuring the multiplicity of sounds that are available to twentieth century musicians.

Whatever variation of the creative approach is used, it is essential for children to develop a mastery of sounds, to enjoy musical work, and to have sufficient opportunities to make an individual contribution.

In the *infant school* music is approached as the continuation of ideal pre-school experience. Songs and rhymes are necessary adjuncts of story, dance and drama. Young children delight in rhythmical work of all kinds, and clapping and tapping are good ways of introducing the learning of songs and simple work with Orff and other percussion instruments. They must be given the opportunity of discovering the variety of sounds produced from wood, metal, glass, and other materials, and of finding the rhythmical possibilities of sounds familiar to them. Whilst infants seem to respond readily to rhythm, pitch appears to be more difficult for them. Some find it easy to sing in tune as early as two years of age, some lose this ability and others never have it at all. A good teacher will help by devising games teaching an awareness of pitch, and giving frequent opportunities for imitation. Any creative work here will be limited to making up simple songs.

The percussion band is a popular musical event at this level and can more appropriately be called recreative than creative. Too often this kind of work can induce regimentation and con-flicts with modern creative methods of infant teaching because the children assume a purely imitative role. A music corner which children can visit informally to experiment with chime-bars, water in bottles, bamboo pipes, or cymbals, as well as with glockenspiels, metallophones, and xylophones, will aid the creative approach.

When children are able to produce simple rhythms, to use percussion confidently and with reasonable accuracy, and to sing within their capabilities, work can progress to a more advanced stage in the *junior school*. A thorough investigation of rhythm leads to the musical possibilities of slogans, proverbs, verse, hand-clapping and finger snapping. Although the emphasis of the work must be creative, often the stimulus of imitation, together with systematic training in visual and aural awareness and in muscular co-ordination, is a pre-requisite for the development of creative expression.

Basic musical activities of the infant school will continue in lower junior school classes—singing, percussion, rhythm practice, listening to music, and a large measure of individual work. As the child develops in his appreciation of music he learns to be more discriminating in his choices and more adventurous in his experimentation. He may, for example, illustrate a story on instruments, composing sounds merry or sad, peaceful or troubled, serene or eerie, to suit the mood of the plot in order to heighten the atmosphere. The use of speech patterns may be continued as a means of developing rhythmic perception and independence.

A growing appreciation of the great composers and of folk music should be fostered gradually, but never forced. Both classical and contemporary music will become more intelligible after classroom experiments in 'home-made' music. There should be frequent opportunities for simple composition of verbal and non-verbal music, and the tape-recorder can be regarded as a musical instrument because effects can be purposefully brought about by deliberate distortion and play-back. Simple composition involves learning to *read* music to some extent. The written symbols of music form a language which must be learnt like other languages, the earlier and less painfully the better. Recorder playing helps considerably in this respect and can be integrated with creative work by an imaginative teacher.

As well as work in conventional notation, the use of approximate notation must not be excluded. Functional symbols, a kind of musical shorthand made up by children, can be valuable, if used in moderation, in helping the process of composition and in introducing the work of contemporary composers.

In the *secondary school* music subject specialists should be able to utilize the results of such creative approaches. At this stage there is a danger that creativity will be submerged in favour of choral singing, instrumental work, competitive and concert performances and unimaginative examination syllabuses.

Children have a feeling for spoken rhythm, and some schools have built upon their participation in chanting (as soccer club supporters do), using knee-clapping and foot-stamping to emphasise rhythm. The rhythms and patterns arising from the chosen words can quickly be transferred to pitched percussion instruments, thus becoming melodic patterns and enabling simple melodies and ensemble music to be created.

But most children at secondary level require something more sophisticated than the Orff kind of approach. If musical interest is to be maintained, especially with boys at the onset of puberty, when the voice is 'breaking', continued participation is essential. Pupils may profitably enjoy pop–folk singing and using guitars to compose simple chordal accompaniments.

At this stage especially, music must be regarded as an integrating force in the curriculum. Wide-ranging projects with a musical connotation can be undertaken. Investigations can be made to discover what type of wood is used for musical instruments, where it comes from, and how it is transported. The lives of composers, various musical instruments, use of music in religious rituals, and numerous other topics form links with the past and present, with Britain and the rest of the world.

No pupil's education is balanced unless he is introduced to and taught to value recognised masterpieces of art and music, the supreme heights of human creative achievement which transcend the boundaries of space and time. Creative listening attitudes must be carefully fostered. There is so much abuse of music as background noise that active and perceptive listening, which can have a creative significance, needs more cultivation than ever. A child must be made aware of what is transcendental in what he hears, whether popular or classical, before he can judge and improve his own creative efforts.

Musical education should be such as to enable each pupil to leave school with sufficient eloquence to contribute to whatever musical environment catches his later interests, and with a sufficient degree of musical literacy to appreciate music in his leisure hours even if he never becomes an active participator in musical activities in his adult life.

Environmental and Social Studies

The eager curiosity of children about the world they live in is a potent spur to learning about those aspects of life which were once conventionally classified as history, geography, and nature study. The community is the world in miniature and provides the basis of a study of man and his relationship with his environment and with other human beings Instances are provided in the locality of every fundamental process, past and present, and teachers must regard the local environment as a lively source of interest for the child. Learning at first hand may be slower than direct instruction from the teacher, because understanding from personal exploration takes time to mature in the mind, but heuristic learning is more satisfying and permanent.

The whole programme in environmental and social studies is aimed, not at amassing knowledge, but at developing the organisation of information and encouraging the child's interest in the environment in which he lives, extending his imagination, giving him techniques by which he can find out information for himself, and providing the motivation for doing so.

Any locality provides many opportunities for pupils to apply and relate their findings in meaningful situations. The basis of the work is exploration and the accurate description and interpretation of the environment. The immediate surroundings of home and school, sights, sound, and people, should be the starting point for work which at secondary level may be classified into more definite subject divisions.

In this work there will be considerable use of language, oral and written. Words, phrases, sentences, labels, connotations, descriptions, and detailed accounts will be used frequently by the children. Clarity in objective description can lead to creative writing. If the explorations into the neighbourhood are sensibly conducted, there will be abundant opportunity for individual interpretation. The recording of the findings can give rise to creative expression in art, both pictorial and craft work, and there is an element of creativity in many questions by children which will form the basis of much of the work. Creative expression can also be communicated in models, collections, the mounting of displays and the presentation of flow charts.

In the *infant school* the movement should be from the familiar to the unknown. Stories about animals, about children in other lands, children of past ages, and workers and their jobs provide a useful supplement to active exploration. Children at this age require concrete experiences, and therefore much of the work must be first hand and self-activating.

The approach must be carefully linked with language, and increased vocabulary must be acquired both incidentally and deliberately. Identification with people in other parts of the country and of the world is the source of a sense of adventure which often results in spontaneous and exiting recording of feeling by young children. A sense of history can be communicated through stories, myths and legends of the local area and interesting legends from all over the world. Stories of great explorers and creators of past and present often have an inspirational quality. These approaches will make infants realise that their own world is merely part of a greater world. When this complements observation of live and local material some very interesting and worthwhile work will result.

As the child enters the *junior school* and grows up within a particular community his personal and social development is being shaped by the neighbourhood. He inherits the way of life, behaviour and characteristics of the locality. His schooling should help him to find a place in his community so that he can enter more fully into its cultural background.

He should be helped to observe and to explore at first hand, and to discover by questioning, in and out of school, the story of the neighbourhood and its relation to wider national and world communities. Teachers must be alive to children's desire for information in order to stimulate their curiosity about the world.

At junior school level the work widens and deepens the child's awareness of the world and increases his battery of skills in interpretation and expression. Active discovery should take place in an appreciation of the wonder of God's creation and an appreciation of its mystical order.

Children at this age begin to demand facts and gradually the story can be replaced by biography, true adventures and achievements. Time should be devoted to the study, not only of persons past and present, but also of ideas and movements. There will be considerably more time spent outside the school, sometimes with carefully planned schedules and purposes, but often at random so that children can develop new interests and follow them up with research. A study of swallows on a local telegraph pole may lead to a wider study of either electricity or migration. A visit to the seaside may set in motion deep inquiry into why the sea appears blue. A country walk may develop interest in maps, photographs, or old documents. In such ways children can often create individual lines of approach.

When the child analyses, with guidance, what he has discovered for himself, he is working creatively. His creative expression can be further extended in the ways he records his knowledge. Not only should he be encouraged to take pride in arranging displays, and presenting collections, but his verbal and written accounts of his discoveries and problem-solving activities can often make refreshing reading and listening. Informal dramatization is also a powerful means of expressing experience in the distant or immediate past. In this way the child can relate in imagination historical actions and characters.

Such an approach leaves the *secondary school* a clear field in which to organise and classify knowledge in subject divisions. History must be regarded as the study of man in chronological time, and geography that of the earth on which he lives. Biology, already referred to, must continue to foster the child's interest in growing and living things. Sociology, the science which studies human society, is only gradually gaining a place in the secondary school curriculum, but would seem to be essential for a comprehensive study of any locality, and how that community has taken shape. The excitement and rewards of first-hand learning and individual investigation should on no account be excluded from secondary school work.

Despite the emphasis on facts and knowledge required for examination purposes, there must be a continuing opportunity for the stimulation and feeding of the child's curiosity, and of helping him to feel a sense of wonder and adventure—essential for the creative process. In addition the work should be designed so that observation, reasoning, and judgment develop constantly in the appreciation of the school locality. This will be possible only if each locality is presented as a rich and varied environment which gives opportunities for meeting individual requirements.

Religious Education

Children growing up in the nineteen-seventies are continually searching for security and certainty in a world of rapidly changing values. This search often takes the form of a question. 'To what end was I born?' No mere intellectual argument can replace the inner transforming realisation that man is created by God. This experience is the very essence of all religion, and throughout his whole history man has been engaged in a constant search for the nature of the Creator and His Creation.

Children best experience God's creative activity when they are given opportunities to be themselves creative. Research has shown that experience is the only effective basis for the development of concepts. Goldman (1964) challenged traditional methods and practices and suggested three stages in the forming of religious concepts: first, the intuitive stage to about 7 years; second, the concrete stage, 7–13; and third, the stage of logical reasoning (13+) when valid concepts could be formed. The investigations of other researchers such as Edwin Cox (1967) and Harold Loukes (1961, 1965) were complementary.

Growing awareness of God as Creator comes gradually from good parent-child and good teacher-child relationships. Recent studies have presented religious education as an interpretation of life in the widest sense and not as an indoctrination into a pattern of belief. This is a much wider interpretation than a system of moral rules and historical facts. Religion is a way of life which affects actions, attitudes and relationships. Therefore religious teaching is concerned with the whole work of the school. Stories and passages from the Bible and other works should be carefully selected and introduced as part of shared experiences with special relevance to the lives of children. God's work as the supreme Creator is clearly set forth in Psalms 19 and 104; and Matthew 10, vv 29–31.

Children can express their views creatively in group activities, and there are opportunities in an integrated curriculum for self-expression through language, art and craft. Religious ideas can be enlarged as children learn more about their surroundings and the world. Biblical events can form subjects for co-operative projects, friezes, drama, dance, mime, and movement, and in this way develop the child's ability to express growing spiritual experiences. The Creator can be perceived in nature, in history, in science, and in mathematics. The children must realise that God is active and that Creation is still going on.

A developing religious concept includes an ability to redefine and re-organise in new ways what is experienced, for this is the essence of creativity. In order to be *spiritually* creative one must participate meaningfully in life, and change from within that in which one participates. Christ Himself was a creative teacher. He more frequently answered questions by provoking new thoughts than by giving ready-made replies. He made the questioners fall back on their own intellectual resources, because He could always draw out unexpected and unconventional responses. He told Nicodemus that to be born again meant to live creatively. Similarly Paul besought the Romans to be transformed by the renewing of their minds (Romans 12, v 2).

The *infant school* stage is very important for religious education. The intuitive emotional knowledge of early childhood goes deeper than any later knowledge gained through the intellect. The age of six has been described as the peak period of child interest in a creative power to which he can relate himself. At this age children think of God in terms of creation (Gesell and Ilg, 1949). The theme of God as Creator can best be understood if the child is helped to see the wonders of creation in objects collected for the nature and adventure corners and in the world around him, in the appreciation of created things, and in the natural world, noting the changes in the seasons, and hearing about creative people. The work must be realistic, within the child's experience, and inspired whenever possible by day-to-day occurrences.

The sense of wonder, an essential requirement of creative expression, is the essence of school worship, and indeed the climax of religious education; its ultimate aim is to lead the pupil to a mystical awareness of the Creator. The difficulties at this stage are the intellectual immaturity of the children and their limited experience of life. The Bible was written for adults, and while some of its stories are very suitable for children, everyday experiences (or Goldman's 'life-themes' modified) are more important in giving a suitable foundation for growing religious concepts. Stories carefully introduced, as part of a shared experience within the school community, will be supplemented by activities such as painting, mime, movement, and later free writing. The infant teacher is concerned less with actual religious knowledge than with the assimilation of values at this important early stage of development, and the gaining of experience as part of the whole educational process.

As the child grows older, society tends to stultify his religious development by denying mystery and wonder. The tendency is to depend less on intuitive recognition and more on analytical thinking. The *junior school* period coincides with the child's 'realistic' stage when fairy tales and fantasy give way, in large measure, to reality. Children are concerned with the concrete, whilst the deeper, abstract religious beliefs are beyond them. The teaching must be relevant to the everyday environment with such activities as will make the understanding of religious concepts possible at a later stage.

Because the child tends to regard everything in his environment as animate, if he is to experience mysticism in his religious beliefs, the teaching he receives must be sensitive to wonder (Fahs, 1965). The main theme will be the life and teaching of Christ, the most rich and creative of lives. Because the change from infancy comes only gradually, there should be continuity in method and approach. Gradually children are ready to relate their experience to certain religious truths, although they cannot yet understand many aspects of the Christian faith. Junior school children begin to learn that Christianity is a social religion, very much concerned with the relationships between people. Along with a growing sense of wonder about certain natural phenomena goes a deepening awareness of people's behaviour to one another. Love of relatives, justice, right and wrong-doing, and suffering (children's own and that of others) are felt acutely.

Children need help to find God in the natural order, and a pattern of life in accordance with truth, beauty and goodness. Religious education must be integrated into the remainder of the curriculum if religion, in the child's view, is to be an integrating force in life. Active creative work will take many forms— scrap-books, friezes, charts, models, dramatisations, anthologies, fictitious eye-witness accounts of Bible happenings, and the writing of simple prayers, which must always be regarded as individual and creative products.

In the upper junior school, children reveal increasing detachment from situations presented to them. They become more concerned with concrete facts and more objective attitudes than with impressions. They have an insatiable curiosity for accurate factual information. Enthusiasms must be fostered unless religious education is to collapse into cynical boredom. Skilful teaching is necessary to overcome the conflict between the natural and supernatural, between reality and the imaginary.

In the *secondary school* stage, religious education, under various names, will usually be taken by specialist teachers. The abrupt change from an integrated curriculum to a specialist subject course can have an adverse effect on the formation of religious concepts. But children of twelve years of age and above are becoming ready for specialistic knowledge, and it is to be hoped that the teachers will build on foundations laid in the primary schools. There is a need for religious education to maintain a separate identifiable existence alongside topic opportunities in the first two secondary years.

Pupils now begin to show a new dimension in their ability to think, and call for a deeper enquiry into the nature of truth. With growing insight into the meaning of the Biblical message, language, and terminology, many will bring a more discerning attitude to the knowledge that they are gaining. No longer will they tolerate a tacit acceptance of inherited beliefs and patterns of behaviour. Decisions arrived at by the pupils must be their own. Religious cliches are particularly abhorrent to them, and as M. C. Jeffreys has pointed out, it is because words can become 'a prison house for ideas as well as a means of enlightenment' that most of the difficulties arising from the communication of the Christian Faith have occurred. Between the ages of thirteen and fifteen childish modes of thought are left behind, and an intellectual tendency emerges. More originality is shown, resulting from a keen consciousness of the basic individualistic character of religious experience. It would seem, then, that religious education has to be creative in order to survive. In reasoned and informed studies of the Bible, language must be clarified, and contemporary translations drawn upon. The life and teaching of Jesus Christ are as relevant as ever, together with a judicious section from the thought and experience of the Biblical authors and also the writings of later Christian writers.

Discussions and activities are all needed to help the pupil clarify his own thought. Research has shown that older pupils enjoy and find meaning in prayers composed by themselves (Jersild, 1954). It is much to be deplored if syllabuses, fashioned to meet external examinations, result in the stultifying of natural religious concept formation.

Comparative religion as it is presented in the past and present does not often lend itself to a truly creative approach, as it often becomes a matter of film descriptions, or sound-strip information. These deal with aspects of other community religions which are clear enough for children to observe and record without their probing deeper or getting involved emotionally. Fortunately a new form of teaching, phenomenology, is gaining favour. This method is to take key phrases common to all religions, such as 'I fear', 'I adore', 'I pray', and 'It is a mystery'. Pupils are shown how each idea operates in the religions, and the work is linked to poetry, drama, and art. They are then encouraged to create their own stories, poems, prayers, ceremonies, mimes, dances, art, and craft. It is clear that there are exciting possibilities for creative work in this approach.

If religious education is presented creatively, throughout all the school stages, with reverence, relevance, simplicity, and depth, the result will be a deepening of religious consciousness, and an appreciation of the wider aspects of the human situation. It is only by learning creatively that a child can acquire lasting beliefs, a reverence for human life, and a respect for individual and group rights.

Organisation of the Curriculum

Although the curriculum areas have been studied separately with regard to their creative potential and methodology, it was emphasised that these disciplines integrate to a considerable extent. Before discussion on the curriculum is terminated, thought must be given to the organisation of the work. Creative expression is possible in the traditional classroom situation in which subjects follow consecutively in a well-ordered fashion, but it is more likely to occur where there is a flexible time-table and when work becomes progressively more integrated. The 'egg box' situation, with every pupil in his place, and where teaching was conducted according to a rigid routine, is giving way to situations in which the teacher guides the children in instructive environments and trains them how to learn for themselves. This freer and more flexible approach takes the form of individual work, small and large group work, discovery situations, topics, projects and team teaching.

Whereas classes were previously grouped according to age or ability, groups are now largely determined by interest, friends, linguistic ability, and sociometric devices. Further variety is added because teachers differ in the extent to which they pursue group teaching. Some group all day for all purposes, some group part of the time, and others group only occasionally. Teachers enthusiastic about group teaching report that children have more turns at activity, more responsibility, more opportunity to work at their own pace, and more experience in social attitudes and social skills. It is evident that in the 'interacting' group system children have an opportunity to experience more types of response than in the 'co-acting' whole-class system where they respond only to the teacher. It would seem, too, that the group system is more 'natural' in that children split up spontaneously into relatively small groups, and only very rarely play in groups of 30 or 40.

The most significant advantage of the group system that has emerged is in the stimulating and creative work attempted. Children learn best what they discover for themselves and groups can be organised for research according to the children's interests. Many opportunities can be arranged for reading, listening, experimenting, interviewing, writing, acting, modelling, problem-solving, evaluating situations, formulating conclusions and social activities such as leading, following, contributing, co-operating, and discussing. This type of learning would seem to be the best possible preparation for the child's future life because nearly all jobs require the ability to work in small groups or departments. Whatever the method and extent of the group method, the teacher's role will be more exacting than that required of him in traditional class-teaching. He must give help and advice where needed and ensure continuity and relevance. His guidance, however, must not be so excessive as to rob the work of its spontaneity. He must ensure suitable standards of work, stimulate the imagination, train the pupils in searching for accurate information and in their reporting and recording activities. He will need to organise periods of class-teaching and discussion in order to explain difficult aspects, basic knowledge and specific skills required in various activities. Above all, he will need to be an expert in human relationships, developing the adjustment of individuals and social interaction within the groups.

The project method, influenced by the work of Froebel and Dewey, was introduced by the pragmatists in the U.S.A. before World War I and defined by its early pioneers as 'wholehearted purposeful activity in a social environment' (Kilpatrick), and as 'a problematic act carried to completion in its natural setting' (Stevenson). Its many interpretations range from publishing a school magazine to focussing work over a considerable period on one topic or centre of interest, and it is widely used in both primary and secondary schools. The advantages of such an approach are significant in stimulating the creative process. Purpose is given to school work, and while the objective of a class lesson is immediate, that of a project is more remote in that it extends over a period of time and demands continuous and purposeful work calling for initiative and tenaciousness of effort. The work becomes significant for children, and the emphasis becomes qualitative rather than quantitative. The greater the involvement in choice of work and planning, the more committed pupils are to the successful carrying out of plans, and the more satisfaction they will find in the work. The project method is spontaneous and responsive to the unfolding situation. It evolves as the work proceeds in individual or group tasks, and calls for co-operation between teacher and child and between child and child. The method also correlates subjects, makes a flexible time table necessary, and helps children to recognise the unity of knowledge. The teacher's work is to stimulate and guide where necessary, to create enthusiasm—and also to decide when a particular project has gone on long enough.

Team teaching has developed in recent years, particularly in the early years of secondary education. In its simplest form a master-teacher introduces a wide topic to a large number of pupils of a particular year or age group in the presence of other teacher-members of the team. In turn, these teachers pursue material of particular interest to them with pupils in smaller groups. At the end of a particular 'topic' or 'project', a demonstration takes place in which every group benefits from everyone else's research and effort.

This approach effects changes not only in the curriculum, but also in the relationship of subjects and their specialist teachers. The initiative comes usually from an enterprising and progressive headmaster, or from a group of teachers who find they have enough in common to be able to work together profitably. Teachers as group leaders give the benefit of their experience and a framework must be a flexible one so that the creative energies if the team are mobilised. For creative expression there must be an atmosphere of genuine democracy within the groups. Differences of opinion and their frank expression are valuable so that the group can organise its internal relationships and work as a small team within the larger one. Team-teaching will play a prominent part in schools in the future because it provides the experimental framework within which most of the current curricular reforms can be incorporated.

In every curriculum area, and in whatever framework of organisation that is in operation, the onus of learning must shift as far as possible from the instructor to the pupil himself. If a child is encouraged to think independently and imaginatively he will bring personal qualities to any work he does, and will obtain self-fulfilment in creative expression.

Training the Creative Teacher

The most creatively constructed curriculum will be fruitless unless teachers are trained to work and to adapt it intelligently. New approaches require not only changes in method and materials, but also a new outlook on the part of the teacher himself. To secure creative pupils it is necessary to develop teachers who are thoroughly trained in a variety of skills necessary for the fostering of creative and productive thinking.

In recent years teacher-training has undergone considerable criticism. The organisational pattern is still based largely on a system in which colleges of education prepare students for non-selective schools, and university departments of education (U.D.E.s) for selective schools. This pattern cannot remain rigid much longer and modifications are being made by the creation of middle schools, by the requirements of the comprehensive system, and by the expansion of post-graduate training and the B.Ed. degree in the colleges of education. The James Committee, which has recently undertaken a major review of teacher taining, has examined, in particular, the content of courses, the feasibility of educating uncommitted students alongside intending teachers, and the role of colleges of education, the polytechnics, and universities.

Its report (*Teacher Education and Training*, published by H.M. Stationery Office, 1972) advocates the demolition of the monotechnic system and replacing it by a First Cycle, in which students aim to gain a Higher Education Diploma; a Second Cycle of professional training which impels intending teachers towards graduate status and re-appraises the probationary year; and a Third Cycle in which in-service training is given top priority. This is particularly desirable at a time when so much educational practice is in a state of transition. If the report is interpreted and implemented wisely, barriers should be broken down between school disciplines, between the primary and secondary sectors, and between schools and colleges. In addition, there should be greater appreciation of curriculum development and a more adventurous use of all educational resources.

The task of training a creative teacher is not an easy one. Much of the difficulty comes from the students' own school experiences. The goal held out to them was a place in a college or a university, to be won as the product of successful formal teaching. Accordingly, as future teachers, students all too often expect to teach in the same way as they themselves were taught. Their attitude to learning has become stereotyped in regard to the formality of ideas, and the teaching example that they should follow will often be impressed upon them by a thorough but formal ex-teacher turned tutor.

It is obvious that future teachers must acquire a basic body of knowledge in various fields, and also professional teaching skills. But the aim must be higher still. By the end of his course, the student should have cultivated a self-critical appraisal of teaching, a flexibility to enable him to cope with change, and a wide vision on which to base professional judgment. The educated student should be able to think and act for himself, and also to co-operate as a useful member of a team. He will have a good academic background, a realisation of social duty, professional expertise, and the necessary personal qualities of integrity and sincerity. Not least. he will become alive to his own creative abilities, so that he can help children to realise their own creative potential. It is doubtful whether the traditional methods in higher education will enable young people to develop on these lines. In the colleges an atmosphere must be created which is both secure and stimulating and in which students can not only co-ordinate knowledge and skills but also explore, challenge and express opinions.

All tutors concerned with teacher-training must make a significant effort to bring the schools, colleges and university departments of education much closer together than in the past. The traditional method of doing this—the school practice—remains of supreme importance today and should prepare for the future as well as reflect the present. The Department of Education and Science circular 24/66 describes the relationship between colleges and schools as the most important factor affecting the quality of training given to intending teachers.

Existing departmental organisation within many colleges, and a too rigid preparation for infant, junior, or secondary work, has sometimes led to the partial neglect of some studies. Subject and education departments often have not accepted direct responsibility for certain essential bodies of knowledge (the neglect of the teaching of reading is the prime example). Colleges and training departments are gradually filling in these gaps. In the general move away from the formal class-teaching situation in many schools, arrangements are made for students to visit schools at times other than the school practice periods. When given the opportunity to concentrate on a small group of children, students are much better able, not only to control their teaching, but also to learn about child and group behaviour. Several students can work together in the same class, and can learn much from discussion as well as from observation and practical application. Study group practice in which tutors, students and teachers co-operate harmoniously as a team can have a very beneficial influence on students preparing for their future career.

The use of video-tapes, films, and closed-circuit television are useful as a preliminary or supplement to observing children working creatively by themselves or in groups. Tutors and students could work together, observing and discussing recorded materials, the interesting sections of which could be repeatedly shown if necessary. Students who have shared in classroom experiences recorded on film or tape have commented favourably on their value. In this way, as well as in direct classroom experience, students discover unsuspected potential in children, and, in helping children to fulfil it, discover their own latent creative capacities also.

This co-operation can also be transferred from the schools to the colleges. School-children and their teachers can be invited into a college and use its facilities in company with a group of students and their teachers in order to appreciate each other's work.

A college or university brings to any area a large body of well-qualified teachers, building resources, sports facilities and a library. These should play an important part in the professional life of the local teaching community. The tutors can become members of teacher committees, and can attend teachers' centres where they can discuss and lecture. Joint appointments as college tutor-teacher advisers can be made and link even more closely the work of the colleges and the schools.

Much is already done in this direction by colleges and faculties of education where lecturers are holding courses for working teachers. The overlap between qualified teachers and teachers-in-training must also be extended and the arrangements for the probationary year made less haphazard so that initial and in-service training merge happily into one another. This first year out of college could well be regarded as an extension of initial training.

Colleges and university departments of education must re-consider their role repeatedly in the future. In educating teachers for the twenty-first century, they must educate for adaptability. Changes in teacher-training will reflect changes both in the education system and in the fabric of society. On the other hand, traditional values will need to be preserved, and the urge for change must be balanced by the realisation of what must be kept unchanged. The task of training creative teachers is particularly difficult in a time of great and rapid social change, and students moulded largely by a convergent process will emerge as the creative teachers of tomorrow only if their tutors regard instruction as a mere *part* of their function. They must be concerned also with the development of personality, individual aspiration, and a spirit of adventure in their students, and with a genuine concern for the progress of the schools to which their students are going to devote their future careers.

References

BERNSTEIN, B. 'Social Class and Linguistic Development: A theory of social learning'. In HALSEY, A. H., ANDERSON, A., and FLOUD, J. (eds.) *Education, Economy and Society*. New York: Free Press, 1961.

CHASE, A. E. *Famous Artists of the Past: A young people's guide to great masters*. London: Macdonald, 1964.

COX, E. *Sixth Form Religion*. London: S.C.M. Press, 1967.

DEUTSCH, C. 'Environment and Perception'. In DEUTSCH, M., KATZ, I., and JENSEN, A. (eds.) *Social Class, Race and Psychological Development*. New York: Holt, Rinehart and Winston, 1968.

FAHS, S. L. *Worshipping Together with Questioning Minds*. Boston, Mass.: Beacon Press, 1965.

FANTINI, M. D., and WEINSTEIN, G. *The Disadvantaged: Challenge to education*. New York: Harper, 1968.

GESELL, A., and ILG, F. *Child Development*. New York: Harper, 1944.

GOLDMAN, R. J. *Religious Thinking from Childhood to Adolescence*. London: Routledge, 1964.

GRIGSON, J., and GRIGSON, G. *Shapes and Stories*. London: John Baker, 1964.

HARRIS, R. J. 'The Only Disturbing Feature'. *The Use of English*, **XVI**, 1965 (197–202).

HOLME, B. *Looking at Drawings*. London: Studio Vista, 1964.

HUGHES, T. (ed). *Here Today*. London: Hutchinson, 1962.

LABAN, R. *Principles of Dance and Movement Notation*. London: Macdonald and Evans, 1956.

LEES, A. *Carl Orff*. London: Calder, 1956.

LOUKES, H. *Teenage Religion*. London: S.C.M. Press, 1961.

LOUKES, H. *New Ground in Christian Education*. London: S.C.M. Press, 1965.

MACLEAN, C., and MACLEAN, M. *Looking at Pictures*. London: Purnell, 1970.

MEILACH, D. Z. *Creating Art from Anything*. London: Pitman, 1971.

MILNE, A. A. *When We were Very Young*. London: Methuen, 1924.

MILNE, A. A. *Now We are Six*. London: Methuen, 1927.

RIESSMAN, F. *Helping the Disadvantaged Pupil to Learn More Easily*. Englewood Cliffs, N.J.: Prentice-Hall, 1962.

SCHOOLS COUNCIL. *Curriculum Innovation in Practice*. London: H.M.S.O., 1968.

SCHOOLS COUNCIL. *Mathematics in Primary Schools* (Curriculum Bulletin No. 1). London: H.M.S.O., 1965.

SLADE, P. *Child Drama*. London: University of London Press, 1954.

TURNER, H. W. 'The Phenomenology of Religion'. A.T.C.D.E. Divinity Section *Bulletin*, **8**, 1969.

WAIN, J. (ed.) *Anthology of Modern Poets*. London: Hutchinson, 1963.

WILKINSON, A. M. 'Research on Formal Grammar'. *N.A.T.E. Bulletin* **1**, 1964 (24–6).

WRIGLEY, J. 'The Schools Council'. In BUTCHER, H. J., and PONT. H. B. (eds.) *Educational Research in Britain 2*. London: University of London Press, 1970.

WOLLMAN, M., and GRUGEON, D. *Happenings*. London: Harrap, 1964.

Further Reading

ALLEN, G. *Social Studies in the Primary School*. London: Macmillan, 1960.

ALTMAN, E. 'Group Study in the College of Education'. *Forum*, **11**, 1969.

ARNOLD, P. J. *Education, Physical Education and Personality Development*. London: Heinemann, 1969.

BERNSTEIN, B. 'Aspects of Language and Learning in the Genesis of Social Process'. *Journal of Child Psychology and Psychiatry*, **1**, 4, 1961.

BOULIND, H. F. (ed.) *Physics*. Harmondsworth: Penguin, 1966.

BOWMAN, M. E. *Romance in Arithmetic*. London: University of London Press, 4th edition, 1969.

BRITTAIN, W. L. *Creativity and Art Education*, Washington, D.C.: National Art Education Association, 1969.

BROWN, M., and PRECIOUS, N. *The Integrated Day in the Primary School*. London: Ward Lock Educational, 1968.

BRUCE, G. *Secondary School Examinations*. Oxford: Pergamon Press, 1968.

BULL, N. J. *Moral Education*. London: Routledge, 1969.

CHILNER, P. *Improvised Drama*. London: Batsford, 1967.

CLEGG, A. *The Excitement of Writing*. London: Chatto and Windus, 1954.

COLLEGIATE FACULTY OF EDUCATION, University College of North Wales. *Language Project: Final report*. Bangor: University College of North Wales, 1969.

COLHAM, J. B. 'An Experiment in School Practice'. *Education for Teaching*, **64,** 1966.

DAVIS, E. C. and WALLIS, E. L. *Toward Better Teaching in Physical Education*. Englewood Cliffs, N.J.: Prentice-Hall, 1961.

DOWDESWELL, H. F. (ed.) *Biology*. Harmondsworth: Penguin, 1966.

DUNSTAN, S. *Principles of Chemistry*. New York: Van Nostrand, 1969.

EASON, T. W. 'What should be taught in Colleges of Education'. *Times Educational Supplement*, 2811, 4 April 1969.

FIELD, D. *Change in Art Education*. London: Routledge 1970.

FLETCHER, H. (ed.) *Mathematics for Schools*. Reading, Mass., and London: Addison-Wesley, 1970.

GARWOOD, K. 'The Colleges and In-service Training'. *New Education*, October 1968.

GLENISTER, S. H. *The Technique of Craft Education*. London: Harrap, 1968.

GOLDMAN, R. J. 'Researches in Religious Thinking'. *Educational Research*, **6,** 2, 1964.

HILLIARD, F. H. 'Universities and the Education of Teachers'. *Educational Review*, 21 February 1964.

HOLBROOK, D. *English for the Rejected*. London: Cambridge University Press, 1964.

JAHODA, G. 'The Development of Children's Ideas about Country and Nationality'. *British Journal of Educational Psychology*, **XXXIII**, 2, 1963.

JEVONS, F. R. *The Teaching of Science*. London: Allen and Unwin, 1969.

KAGE, B. *Participation in Learning: A progress report on some experiments in the training of teachers*. London: Allen and Unwin, 1969.

KING, W. H. 'The Development of Scientific Concepts in Children'. *British Journal of Educational Psychology*. **33**, 3, 1963.

LAWRENCE, E., ISAACS, N., and RAWSON, W. *Approaches to Science in the Primary School*. Harlow: Educational Supply Association, 1960.

LOUKES, H. *New Ground in Christian Education*. London: S.C.M. Press, 1965.

LOVELL, K. *Growth of Basic Mathematical and Scientific Concepts in Children*. London: University of London Press, 1961.

MARSH, L. G. *Children explore Mathematics*. London: A. and C. Black, 1969.

MARTIN, N., BRITTON, J., and ROSEN, H. 'Abilities to Write'. *New Education*, October, 1966.

MATTEL, E. L. *Meaning in Crafts*. Englewood Cliffs, N.J.: Prentice-Hall, 1965.

NISBET, J. D., and ENTWISTLE, N. J. *Educational Research Methods*. London: University of London Press, 1970.

PAYNTER, J., and ASTON, P. *Sound and Silence*. London: Cambridge University Press, 1970.

PETERSON, A. D. C 'Who teaches the Teacher?' *University Quarterly*, Summer 1970.

POWELL, B. *English through Poetry Writing*. London: Heinemann, 1968.

PYM, D. *Free Writing*. London: University of London Press (for University of Bristol School of Education), 1956.

REID, L. A. *Meaning in the Arts*. London: Allen and Unwin, 1970.

RICHARDS, M. P., and ROSS, H. E. 'Development Changes in Children's Drawings'. *British Journal of Educational Psychology*, **37**, 1, 1967.

RICHARDSON, E. *Group Study for Teachers*. London: Routledge, 1967.

Science in Primary Schools. London: H.M.S.O. (Pamphlet 42), 1961.

SEALEY, L. G. W. *The Creative Use of Mathematics in the Junior School.* Oxford: Blackwell, 1960.

SHAPLIN, J. T., and OLDS, H. T. *Team Teaching.* New York: Harper, 1965.

SHIELDS, J. B. *The Gifted Child.* Slough: National Foundation for Educational Research, 1968.

SILKS, G. B. *Creative Dramatics, An Art for Children.* New York: Harper, 1958.

THOULESS, R. T. *Map of Educational Research.* Slough: National Foundation for Educational Research, 1969.

VIGOTSKY, L. *Thought and Language.* New York: John Wiley, 1960.

WARWICK, D. W. *Team Teaching.* London: University of London Press, 1971.

D

CHAPTER FIVE

Measuring and Predicting Creativity

An interesting by-product of the movement to identify factors in creativity has been the development, in recent years, of ingenious means to measure these factors, and much effort has been expended in the search for reliable predictors of creativeness. Most of these efforts have been only relatively successful, because though intelligence and creativity are related, they are constituted of overlapping sets of abilities. Tests available are designed to measure the essential ingredients of creativity—flexibility, originality, sensitivity, spontaneity and fluency in response to problems and ideas.

Creativity tests measure those characteristics important for school and life which are not identified and measured at present by conventional I.Q. and aptitude tests. They are designed to elicit novel responses and unusual solutions to problems. Creative thinking tests are not so much concerned with whether answers are right or wrong as whether responses are fluent or restricted, divergent or conventional. Their distinctive characteristic is that the testee must usually produce a number of answers rather than select one correct answer, and is called upon to produce multiple responses rather than one accurate one. Individuals whose special abilities are of a productive rather than a reproductive nature do well in the tests.

Guilford (1956) formed a model of the structure of intelligence, distinguishing between the 'content' of thought, the ways of thinking or 'operations', and the 'products' of thought. His interrelated system recognised 120 separate mental abilties, each of which he claimed may be measured. Many of these, particularly the divergent thinking 'operations', were not tapped by conventional I.Q. tests. He and his colleagues, working with Air Cadets and student officers, devised 53 separate tests. After considerable experiment they were satisfied that they had identified and statistically differentiated at least 14 specific factors in creativeness.

Getzels and Jackson (1962), inspired by Guilford's new instrument of measuring intelligence, utilised in their study a group of five measures, some of which had been constructed by Guilford and Cattell. Getzels and Jackson found positive but low correlations between measures of divergent thinking and intelligence. The five measures they used were: word associations; uses for common objects; hidden shapes; endings for uncompleted fables; and making up problems.

Barron (1961) used eight tests in seeking to measure originality among a group of Air Force captains. His findings indicated that the correlation of intelligence and creativity over the whole range of ability was $+ \cdot 40$, but that the correlation among individuals with I.Q.s over 120 was only $+ \cdot 10$.

Torrance and his colleagues (1962), working at the University of Minnesota, attempted to modify a number of the tests for elementary school children and also produced a number of tests of their own. They adapted Guilford's 'Unusual Uses of Objects' test, and developed a battery of questions involving problems, improvements, consequences and situations. They then produced two non-verbal tests, one presenting a geometrical figure and asking the testee to sketch objects using the figure as the main element of design, and the other making a study of non-essential details which a child introduces in producing drawings of simple objects. R. J. Goldman (1966) in a comprehensive article in *Educational Research* asserted that the Minnesota tests will require considerable modification and adaptation for use in Great Britain. Torrance's findings replicated those of Getzels and Jackson, and he reported a positive but low correlation between intelligence and creative powers as represented by tests of ideational fluency, spontaneous flexibility, inventiveness, and constructiveness.

Wallach and Kogan (1965), who had questioned the evidence produced by Getzels and Jackson, investigated the relationship between creativity and intelligence. They proceeded to construct new divergent thinking tests based on a conceptualisation of creativity similar to Mednick's (1962). Their investigation, described in *Modes of Thinking in Young Children* (1965), showed that they obtained scores on three of the Weschler Intelligence Scale tests, on two aptitude tests, on five scholastic achievement tests, and on ten tests of creativity (verbal and non-verbal) from 70 boys and 81 girls in the fifth grade of a public elementary school in New England. The average age of the pupils was 10 years 7 months. The data was obtained in individual situations, with no time limit, and in a friendly and relaxed atmosphere. The responses were scored both for total number and for uniqueness. Correlating their results with measures of intelligence, Wallach and Kogan concluded that their 'construct' of creativity possessed an internal consistency similar to the range of general intelligence but clearly independent of it. While both the measures of intelligence and measures of creativity were separately distinguished, the correlation between the measures was low.

A study of a group of gifted children in two cities in the north of England was made by Lovell and Shields (1967). The ages of the children ranged from 8 years 5 months to 11 years 7 month. Measures of intellectual ability were obtained by Scale tests, by a number of tests of logical thinking designed by Piaget, and by a number of mathematical tests. The divergent thinking test consisted of problems concerning hidden shapes, word association, uses of objects, incomplete fables, and making-up numerical problems. These tests were administered in the pupils' own schools, in a relaxed atmosphere and, with the exception of the hidden shapes test, without a time limit.

Lovell and Shields compared the scores gained on the creativity tests not only with intelligence test scores, but also with those gained on the tests of logical thinking and mathematical ability. They discovered the existence of a strong intellective component, common to all the tests. They were of the opinion that the creativity tests did not measure intellectual abilities entirely independent of those measured by conventional I.Q. tests, and that a number of factors overlapped statistically. Nevertheless, despite a clear common factor, there was evidence to suggest the existence of creative thinking abilities.

Other recent researchers have followed a similar pattern with variations in the correlation between intelligence and creativity. Hasan and Butcher (1966) found a high correlation ($\cdot$74) in their research with Scottish school-children, and Ginsberg and Whittemore (1968) reported a correlation of $\cdot$60 in their Australian sample. Dacey, Madaus and Allen (1969) found the highest of nine correlations to be $\cdot$17 when they studied the relationship of three I.Q. levels in three diverse areas. The same three researchers, in another study of 182 Irish adolescents from suburban Dublin

(1969), found that divergent thinking and intelligence emerged almost as separate dimensions. They found a separation also between the verbal and non-verbal divergent thinking measures, although this was not as clear as that between divergent thinking and intelligence.

Although all these researchers have made important contributions to our knowledge of the relationship between creativity and intelligence, and have improved the techniques for predicting divergent thinking as a 'probability function', yet until there is a clear definition of terms and an isolation between factors such as scoring procedures, test situations (group or individual, speed versus power testing), and instructions, the true relationship between intelligence and divergent thinking factors cannot be determined with complete assurance.

Before an attempt is made to evaluate and justify measuring creativity, it is advantageous to outline a number of examples of the open-ended questions which are characteristic of the creativity tests so far produced.

USES OF OBJECTS
The testee is asked to think and write down as many uses as he can for common objects such as a pin, rope, button, piano, wheelbarrow, paper. Marks are awarded for number of uses, and additional marks given for unusual uses. The scoring of these responses pose a problem. The tester must decide whether he is to score all responses, possible and impossible, whether marks are to be adjudged for quality of the suggestions as well as number, and whether there can be a scale of originality.

STORIES
The testee is sometimes required:
a to compose different endings to incomplete stories;
b to produce titles to go with a brief story;
c to give interpretation of anagrams; or
d to write brief stories from illustrations.
These are rated for originality.

ASSOCIATION OF WORDS
The testee is asked:
a to give as many different meanings as possible for common

words (the ability to move freely from one context to another is a good indication of potential creativity);

b to produce words beginning with a certain letter and ending in another stated letter.

It would seem that richness of vocabulary derived from an educated background and wide reading would strongly influence results in these tests.

SHAPES

a The testee is asked to take a shape such as a square or circle, and to use it as a base for elaborating objects and drawings.

b Given certain basic materials, the testee is required:

    (i) to improvise with common objects such as modelling material;

    (ii) to form mosaics—which are assessed for unusual patterns;

    (iii) to find hidden shapes (i.e. discern hidden geometric shapes in a complex diagram).

MAKING-UP PROBLEMS

a Paragraphs are presented, each containing numerical statements within the experience of the testee who is expected to make up a number of problems arising from the situations.

b A brief description is given of an everyday situation and the testee is required to pose interesting problems.

IDEATIONAL FLUENCY

Sometimes the testee is asked to suggest consequences of highly improbable events, e.g.

a The sea everywhere raises its level by 10 feet.

b The earth suddenly moves a million miles nearer the sun.

c All human beings suddenly become deaf.

d Clever human beings land in large numbers from another planet.

Responses from these tests are scored for fluency (the total number of responses accumulated), flexibility (the number of movements from one category of response to another), originality (the unusualness of the responses produced), and humour. In nearly all these tests no time limit is set, and it is essential that they be conducted in an atmosphere of friendliness.

A recent development has been the construction of tests responses to which may be assessed in terms of degree of correctness.

These tests are open-ended, but for them correct solutions (and therefore incorrect solutions, also) exist. The words-in-context tests (Cook, Heim, and Watts, 1963) were intended primarily as group tests of general reasoning with a verbal bias. They differ from other such tests in that they make use of frequently met real-life situations, demand inductive as well as deductive reasoning, are objectively scorable in that a correct answer exists for each problem, and allow also for *degrees* of rightness and wrongness. The self-judging vocabulary scale (Heim and Watts, 1961) is a test of knowledge rather than reasoning and is open-ended, or multiple choice, or both, according to the wish of the testee. The element of choice is, in itself, an invitation to originality.

It must now be asked to what extent these various tests tap some common function of creativity. It is clear that divergent thinking tests do not measure the same attributes which are tapped by conventional intelligence tests.

'Fluency' and 'originality' do not appear to have much in common, and both have only a small overlap with 'flexibility'. Nevertheless, research suggests that there does exist a common core running through the different tests and making for correlation between them, but this common core appears to make only a small contribution to success in these tests. While these various elements play a harmonious part in the creative process, their diversity makes it very difficult to measure accurately. Because every creative act overpasses the established order in some way and in some degree, the amount of creativity is often a matter of opinion rather than measurement.

Tests are used primarily to enable us to make statements about the future performance of the person taking the test. The ultimate criterion of such a test is its success in predicting an ability or pattern of behaviour at some future time. Because creativeness is difficult to assess, and because in the vast majority of people it is the process rather than the product which is valuable, it is questionable whether divergent thinking tests are of value as predictors of performance. It is a doubtful assumption that an individual's abilities do not change much over a period of time. We know that intelligence can change considerably in certain conditions. It would seem that creativity is also dependent on circumstances and could change substantially over a period.

A test's value as a prediction of creativity depends both on the relationship between the abilities required by the test and on the abilities needed in the situation for which the performance is predicted. As well as analysing the many variables that make up the test performance, one must decide what abilities are most important. Every test should be checked for external validity (i.e. does it measure real behaviour?); internal validity (does it measure what it sets out to measure?); and reliability of results over a period of time, or long term reliability: whether the results remain the same the next week or the next year. Conventional tests of intelligence, attainment and aptitude are likely to fulfil these three requirements and to be good predictors of subsequent academic performance. This is because educational success is judged basically in terms of ability to pass tests and examinations which require the same qualities as predictor tests. Creative performance, on the other hand, does not depend on ability to pass tests. Actually, creativity is often confined and endangered by a test environment.

Creative tests are not fully objective, and depend on the experimenter's subjective assessment of the creative quality in the response. This subjective character will necessarily reduce the reliability of the tests but this is inseparable from the attempt to measure creativity. Originality and fluency can be part determined by statistical techniques assessing the likelihood of a response compared with the norm after examining the responses of a number of testees.

There is no clear evidence that high scores on tests of divergent thinking will be particularly productive of creativity in later life, and Liam Hudson (1966) has questioned the idea that excellence in answering open-ended tests necessarily means the presence of a high degree of creativity. But there is no evidence of the converse, that success in these tests does not lead to later creative performance. The best approach probably is to regard high scores on divergent thinking tests as some indication of a lack of anxiety about non-conforming responses; this is a necessary condition, but it is not sufficient in itself for the production of creative work.

For the teacher in the classroom, tests for creativity may not be practicable or even available. The identification of creative pupils will largely depend on the teacher's role as an observer. Children with high creative potential will probably show some or many of the following characteristics: satisfaction derived from new and different approaches, ability to go beyond facts to discern new implications, persistence and self-discipline, fluency of ideas, ability to find unity in apparent diversity, sensitivity to problems, active imagination, and concern for unsolved problems. They will create original stories, plays, poetry, toys, tunes, and sketches, use materials, words and ideas in new ways, see flaws in things, in-including their own work, will ask many questions and will experiment in order to get answers. A perceptive teacher will make himself aware of the creative potential of his pupils without the aid of tests. But he must never be distracted from his main task, which is to enable all his pupils to reach their creative potential whether or not they show promise of high creativity. Tests can only distinguish various factors complementary to the behaviour patterns classed as 'creative'. They are crude tools which have to be refined in special cultural and social contexts, and statistics must reflect these defined contexts. Only then can such tests be valid for formulating theories of creativity. Despite all the research, it does not appear likely that there will ever be a single, widely-accepted creativity test. A great deal more basic inquiry is necessary before the structure of creativity is clear, or the practical utility of different types of divergent thinking measures can be determined. Meanwhile, the term 'creativity' must be used tentatively as applied to any or all of the tests and to children or adults selected on the basis of them. Already, however, it seems clear that children who achieve high scores on measures of creative thinking abilities differ in fundamental ways from those who score low on such measures. They prefer to learn in creative ways, by explora-tion, experimentation and discovery.

In considering whether the tests will help materially in select-ing personnel for various posts where inventive capability is required, such as scientists, engineers, administrators, planners, politicians, it can only be stated, at this time, that where tests are already used, tests of divergent thinking in conjunction with those of convergent thinking would lead to better selection than was hitherto possible with traditional tests. But too much heed should not be paid to tests for selection purposes because the intellectual tasks in any occupation, especially at professional levels, are very complex. It is unlikely that any one aptitude plays an exclusive role in success in any particular occupation. A combination of different abilities is needed for each selection situation, and the combination may vary from one group of occupations to another, and even within the one occupation. Employers seeking highly creative personnel for posts should not confine their attention to tests of divergent thinking abilities, for many other kinds of abilities contribute to a creative output, depending upon different circumstances.

Tests of divergent thinking nevertheless serve a useful purpose and fully justify their existence. They have rescued the concept of creativity from the realm of mystery and shown it to be subject to study and analysis. They indicate that factors involved in the creative process are identifiable. Their existence provides a safeguard against neglecting the development of divergent-thinking abilities, and they are more objective than even the best observation. The research on these tests has uncovered a body of information which has made educators aware of, and more capable of realising, creative potential. These tests provide a welcome supplement to intelligence tests, and afford another dimension in the concept of giftedness even though they indicate the type rather than the level of future performance. They have already been the means of becoming aware of potentialities that might otherwise have gone unnoticed. Even among their critics, there is some acceptance of the proposition that creative thinking abilities exist, and that, to some degree, they can be measured by tests.

At present, the tests are not used on a large scale in Britain, and this limited use is entirely justified until further research has thrown more light on their purpose and reliability. But interest in American research, which has produced nearly all the tests already available, has served to highlight and publicise the movement towards creative learning and thinking which cannot fail to have a beneficial effect in education.

References

BARRON, F. 'The Disposition towards Originality'. *Journal of Abnormal Psychology*, **32**, 1962.

COOK, J. M., HEIM, A. W., and WATTS, K. P. 'The Words in Context: a new type of verbal reasoning test'. *British Journal of Psychology*, **54**, 1963 (227–37).

DACEY, J., MADAUS, G., and ALLEN, A. 'The Relationship of Creativity and Intelligence in Irish Adolescents'. *British Journal of Educational Psychology*, **39**, 3, 1969.

GETZELS, J. W., and JACKSON, P. W. *Creativity and Intelligence*. New York: John Wiley, 1962

GINSBERG, G. P., and WHITTEMORE, R. G. 'Creativity and Verbal Ability: a direct examination of their relationship'. *British Journal of Educational Psychology*, **38**, 1968.

GOLDMAN, R. J. 'The Minnesota Tests of Creative Thinking'. *Educational Research*, November 1964.

GUILFORD, J. P. 'The Structure of Intellect'. *Psychological Bulletin*, **53**, 1956 (267).

HASAN, P., and BUTCHER, H. J. 'Creativity and Intelligence: a partial replication with Scottish children of Getzels' and Jackson's study'. *British Journal of Psychology*, **57**, 1966.

HEIM, A. W., and WATTS, K. P. 'A Preliminary Study of the Self-judging Vocabulary Scale'. *British Journal of Psychology*, **52**, 1961 (175–86).

HUDSON, L. *Contrary Imaginations*. London: Methuen, 1966.

LOVELL, K., and SHIELDS, J. B. 'Some Aspects of a Study of the Gifted Child'. *British Journal of Educational Psychology*, **37**, 1967.

MEDNICK, S. A. 'The Associative Basis of the Creative Process'. *Psychological Review*, 1962 (220–32).

TORRANCE, E. P. *Guiding Creative Talent*. Englewood Cliffs, N.J.: Prentice-Hall, 1962.

WALLACH, M., and KOGAN, W. *Modes of Thinking in Young Children*. New York: Holt, Rinehart and Winston, 1965.

Further Reading

BURT, C. 'The Psychology of Creative Ability'. *British Journal of Educational Psychology*, **32**, 1962.

BUTCHER, H. J. *Human Intelligence*. London: Methuen, 1968.

BUTLER, J. R. *Occupational Choice*. London: H.M.S.O., 1968.

CLINE, V. B., RICHARDS, J. M., and NEEDHAM, W. E. 'Creativity Tests and Achievement in High-school Success'. *Journal of Applied Psychology*, **47**, 1963.

CROPLEY, A. J., and MASLANY, G. W. 'Reliability and Factorial Validity of the Wallach-Kogan Creativity Tests'. *British Journal of Psychology*, **60**, 3, 1969.

DEBNEY, B. 'Testing Creativity'. *Educational Review*, 21 June 1969.

FLESCHER, I. 'Anxiety and Achievement of Intellectually Gifted and Creatively Gifted Children'. *Journal of Psychology*, **56**, 1963.

FOSS, B. M. *New Horizons in Psychology*. Harmondsworth: Penguin, 1969.

FREEMAN, F. S. *Theory and Practice of Psychological Testing*. New York: Holt, Rinehart and Winston, 3rd edition, 1962.

GOLD, M. J. *Education of the Intellectually Gifted*. Columbus, Ohio: Charles E. Merrill, 1965.

GOSLIN, D. A. *The Search for Ability*. New York: Russell Sage Foundation, 1963.

GUILFORD, J. P. 'Potentiality for Creativity and its Measurement'. In *Proceedings of the 1962 Invitational Conference on Testing Problems*. Princeton, N.J.: Educational Testing Services, 1963.

HEIM, A. W. *Intelligence and Personality*. Harmondsworth: Penguin, 1970.

HUDSON, L. *Frames of Mind*. Harmondsworth: Penguin, 1968.

MADAUS, G. F. 'A Cross-cultural Comparison of the Factor-structure of Selected Tests of Divergent Thinking'. *Journal of Social Psychology*, **73**, 1967.

MAGNUSSON, D. *Test Theory*. Reading, Mass.: Addison-Wesley, 1967.

MARSH, R. W. 'A Statistical Re-analysis of Getzels' and Jackson's Data'. *British Journal of Educational Psychology*, **34**, 1966.

MCHENRY, R. E., and SHOUKSMITH, G. A. 'Creativity, Visual Imagery and Suggestibility: their relationship in a group of ten-year-old children'. *British Journal of Educational Psychology*, **40**, 2, 1970 (154–60).

PAFFARD, M. K. 'Creative Activities and "Peak" Experiences'. *British Journal of Educational Psychology*, **40**, 3, 1970.

RIPPLE, R. E., and MAY, F. B. 'Caution in comparing Creativity with I.Q.' *Psychological Reports*, **10**, 1962.

ROBINSON, J., and BARNES, N. (eds.) *New Media and Methods in Industrial Training*. London: B.B.C. Publications, 1967.

STEIN, M. I. 'Creativity and Culture'. *Journal of Psychology*, 36, October 1953.

SULTAN, E. E. 'A Factorial Study in the Domain of Creative Thinking'. *British Journal of Educational Psychology*, **32**, 1962 (78–82).

TAYLOR, C. W., and HOLLAND, J. L. 'Development and Application of Tests of Creativity'. *Revue of Educational Research*, **32**, 1962.

TORRANCE, E. P. *The Minnesota Studies of Creative Thinking in*

Early School Years. Minneapolis, Minn.: St Paul Bureau of Educational Research, University of Minnesota, 1960.

TORRANCE, E. P. *Torrance Tests of Creative Thinking.* Princeton, N.J.: Personnel Press, 1966.

TORRANCE, E. P. *Rewarding Creative Behaviour.* Englewood Cliffs, N.J.: Prentice-Hall, 1965.

WARD, J. 'An Oblique Factorisation of Wallach and Kogan Correlations'. *British Journal of Educational Psychology,* **37,** 1967.

WILSON, F. T. 'Some Special Ability Test Scores of Gifted Children'. *Journal of Genetic Psychology,* **82,** March 1953.

WILSON, R. C., GUILFORD, J. P., CHRSTENSEN, P. R., and LEWIS, D. J. 'A Factor-analytic Study of Creative Thinking Abilities'. *Psychometrika,* **XIX,** 1954.

WRIGLEY, J. *Measuring the Mind.* Southampton: Southampton University, 1965.

YAMAMOTO, K. *Experimental Scoring Manuals for Minnesota Tests of Creative Thinking and Writing.* Kent, Ohio: Bureau of Educational Research, Kent State University, 1964.

CHAPTER SIX

Creativity and Society

Any small change in a nation's attitude to creativeness can have very beneficial repercussions on its members both corporately and individually. Every person needs help to reach his full potential, not only physically and intellectually, but also creatively, and the awareness of this need is a challenge calling for immediate action. Indeed, creativity can be thought of as self-fulfilment aiming for excellence. Whilst assimilating the culture which he has inherited, and adapting himself to it, man must also preserve his essential individuality. Education must assist the society which nurtures it by inspiring each generation to add to the culture it has received by creating something new; there should be no passive acceptance of what has been handed down from the past. Serious consideration must therefore be given to the extent that non-conforming ideas can be considered as an asset for life in a conforming society. Originality that will be valuable to society, as opposed to irresponsible imaginings and divergence for its own sake, must be based on intelligent far-sightedness. Creativeness must, somehow, be fostered without developing anti-social individualism or eccentricity. Debunking traditional ideas is not necessarily a sign of valuable creativity. The problems of society—its government, its economic structure, its work and its leisure—all call for imaginative and creative solutions.

We have seen that every human being possesses at his own level and degree a creative potential that can be nurtured. The creative activities of children are well-known, and at play they exteriorise their inner life, discovering abilities, investigating their environment and solving problems. The rapidly accumulating body of research available will help to further this creativeness. Ingenious tests have been devised which not only measure creative factors with some degree of reliability, but also note the frequent occurrence of these factors in dissimilar circumstances. Research has not only established and defined creativeness as a personal endowment, and noted clearly-marked stages in its development, it has also discovered much that is of use to educators in bringing out the qualities essential to the realisation of the creative spirit.

Whereas conditions in the past favoured the reception of knowledge rather than self-expression, reproduction rather than production, re-creation rather than original creation, it is now known that schools can do a great deal to promote growth of personality by fostering the creative process in their organisation, in every branch of their curriculum, and in their methodology, aiming at discovery, enjoyment, and independent thought.

In order to be truly effective in methods and practice of teaching free rein must be given to the imagination, and the creative process must have the support of the nation, as well as that of the schools, which are only a reflection of the nation. The world of the near future will demand men with a greater degree of versatility than is needed even today; they must be adaptable not only in the vocational sense, but also in their ability to make full use of leisure.

Technological changes occur so rapidly that entirely new industries are being established within a few years to replace old ones which have survived for decades. In another 25 years there may be no bankers, cobblers, or typists, and very few clerks. Young people commencing their careers in industrial production should expect to learn a new skill at least twice in their lifetime.

Vast problems, national and international, will arise, calling for brave new solutions. World problems such as international peace and the expansion of population concern every nation. Should the 'nuclear deterrent' become an instrument of aggression in the world, human civilisation as known today may well disappear. Even without a third world war, if the world population continues to expand at the present rate many millions will die of famine by A.D. 2025 unless some effective means are devised, not only of increasing food production on a large scale, but also of decreasing the birth rate.

New means of communications have broadened people's horizons, and rapidly emerging nations, brought into contact with more advanced technological societies, create a demand for mutual understanding and respect. Man's inventive and political capacities need to develop further than ever before. Should independent creative thinking spread into every sphere of living, men could discard the old, narrow, restricted ways of thought to the benefit of everyone. Each man has a right to develop in his own way, and every effort must be made for this development.

Increasing technological sophistication has caused many problems, both financial and personal. The significant increase in nervous tension has resulted in a corresponding increase in the number of psychologists and psychiatrists. Many people are living in a state of constant anxiety about their past, present, and future. Children and young people are now exposed to experiences affecting their emotional life to an intensity that has never been experienced before. Murder, violence, and sex are seen daily on television and film. Everyday contact with sickness and death, formerly reserved for special groups of trained people such as nurses, doctors, and policemen, have become the common vicarious experience of all, irrespective of age and emotional development. Many people, for a variety of reasons, find contemporary pressures hostile to security and compassion, because personal well-being is anchored to familiar materialistic symbols. A considerable increase in the amount of research is necessary in order to understand fully these stresses and conflicts.

It is paradoxical that, with the dramatic increase of mass communication, the gulf between young people and their elders has widened and the links between one generation and the next are becoming increasingly weaker. There is much less respect for authority and for accumulated experiences handed down from one generation to another. At the same time there seems to be a growing sense of compassion, especially among young people.

In Western society an emphasis on creativity could eventually counteract the protest, the anti-intellectualism, and the general indifference towards intellectual achievements; for it is reasonable to assume that the problem-solving activities built into any programme designed to stimulate creative thinking are capable of solving many difficulties. The abilities generally required to solve problems of behaviour can be regarded as basically the same as those called for by other problems. Such an approach would be more positive than doing nothing until a crisis demands immediate action, when only externally imposed solutions can be applied. In the field of mental health this is already being done. Instruction is given to patients to prevent personal and behavioural crisis, and to prepare them to meet and cope with future difficulties. In the United States of America, in particular, education programmes called 'sensitivity training' for both children and adults have as their object the understanding of the behaviour of the mind. In this type of training, as in mental hygiene and therapy, the possibility of acquiring skills through practice is recognised. It would seem that a personal adjustment could be more easily achieved as part of a widespread movement towards solving personal problems in creative ways depending upon divergent thinking and evaluation.

The economic progress of the Western world has been revolutionised by such epoch-making inventions as the automobile, the radio, and television, and it was the original thinking of a few individuals that was responsible. This originality, of course, has as its basis knowledge derived from the work of countless others. But it was individual perception of this knowledge that gave birth to the inventions. The stability of Western economy depends on such inventive progress and can only be maintained by corresponding inventiveness when and as the occasion demands. Developments spring from the creative thinking of individuals. In future the economy will need the dedicated efforts of many more creative minds free to advance in the direction in which their inspiration will lead them.

Already, in some industries, employees are rewarded for ingenious ideas and suggestions. Management should everywhere publicise the giving of special awards for useful divergent thinking even though the firm cannot immediately avail itself of the ideas thus obtained. Ultimately this may provide solutions to important problems.

At present Britain is faced with vital issues. There is a never-ending race between wages and prices, unrest among youth, increase in crime, industrial troubles arising from unemployment, automation and technological advance, and difficulties in relations with other countries. Such difficulties will never be overcome without creative thinking, leading to solutions both new and courageous. For such problems there is seldom only one correct answer. If this fact were widely recognised, many avenues of thinking could be opened up that otherwise would never be explored, and the stagnation which has prevailed whilst men wait for one correct solution (so seldom emerging) avoided.

The school is an interpreter and a moulder of society and is itself a society in miniature. Hitherto, education has been provided by handing down from one generation to another a body of knowledge and a variety of skills. In a technological society, however, this concept will have to be modified because the most valuable person will not be the one who has absorbed knowledge and mastered techniques, but he who is himself creative and inventive, or else sufficiently flexible in mind to learn quickly, and perhaps adapt and modify new techniques devised by others. Our changing industries and commercial system depend on people being able to continue learning new skills rather than absorb uncritically a body of static knowledge or master traditional skills. The nature of one component ability will depend upon the kind of operation intended, the mind of information supplied, and the activity to be applied because of the information. To regard education as a means of training the intellect only is old-fashioned; new information about the creative process gives an educational objective which is much richer and more comprehensive. From this knowledge we deduce that generalised intellectual skills can exist in addition to specific skills. A wider acceptance of the concept of creativity would accelerate the effort to give children the opportunity to exercise general skills. They can be guided to realise the nature of these skills, and so to become aware of those which they are likely to develop. Every individual should be expected to develop a minimal level in all skills which have personal and social value, and should be encouraged to proceed to a more advanced level in those for which he has a special aptitude. Gifts make themselves known in many different ways; and the traditional method of assessing and selecting them on the basis of intelligence and attainment tests which favour the conformer often misses the potentially creative individual and sometimes even the genius. There is considerable evidence to show that marks scored in tests of the components of fluency and flexibility can be increased as the result of a course on creative thinking (e.g. Osborn, 1957; Maltzman, Simon, Raskin, and Licht, 1960; Torrance, 1962; and de Bono, 1967). Probably no subject or course is without its opportunities to teach creatively; and all learning will be more exciting, thrilling and meaningful with imaginative teaching. In this system self-initiated activity on the part of the learner is encouraged, and unique as well as conforming achievements are rewarded. Effective learning is characterised by personal expression, personal experience, and personal discovery, and the educator accepts what the learner produces while trying to enlarge his background and enhancing his skills.

Such an atmosphere of changed attitudes and discovery can make possible the replacement of old values by new, and those individuals can develop who will use their own creativeness in accordance with the pressing needs of existing circumstances. Such a fully educated society will be more capable of planning its own path ahead than any previous society, which has only reacted passively to overwhelming socio-economic pressures.

A technological civilisation will, for the first time, make it possible for the whole of society, as opposed to an educated elite, to enjoy an extended leisure. The great majority of our forefathers were so busy in ensuring that they were housed, clothed and fed, that they could think of nothing else. Organised technology and automation have now brought us nearer the stage when leisure time and working hours will be equal.

It is significant that the Electical Construction Engineers of New York have already achieved a 25-hour week, and it is quite conceivable that in Britain the average working hours will eventually be reduced to six hours a day, four days a week, with at least six weeks' holidays in the year. It is evident that the problems of training for leisure is going to become as important as training for work.

The varieties of leisure are endless. S. P. Parker (1967) distinguished three main types. The extension pattern was one where non-work and work activities have a close connection. This type included almost exclusively professional and academic people, whose work satisfied them and was the central interest in their lives. The neutrality pattern included clerks and semi-skilled workers, whose leisure was the central interest of their lives because of the monotonous nature of their work. The opposition pattern was usually found amongst manual and unskilled labourers. Their work was not the central interest of their lives and was sharply separated from their leisure—their time for recuperation. There are doubtless many variation patterns, and leisure has individual significance for every person.

The educational implications are evident. Society must aim at the development of the capacity to enjoy experience for its own sake, making sure that leisure enriches a person's life, and does not reduce him to a standardised and bored unit in the mass-produced values in the world of mass media. At present, many agencies are working to provide opportunities for all kinds of artistic and physical recreation. The Arts Council and the Central Council of Physical Recreaction are well established, and a network of drama, music and other societies is spread throughout Britain but there is insufficient co-ordination of effort between the forces at work to meet an enormous potential demand. In the Youth Service, often the very people who need most to be involved in Youth Club activities are not, for various reasons, drawn to it. In the adult world, too, for the majority leisure has meant inertia and boredom, relieved only by the short-term excitements and stimulants of mass entertainment and commercially manufactured sensations. 'Betting, bingo, and booze' comprise the leisure of many. The capacity to be absorbed in an activity for its own sake is the supreme antidote to boredom.

This important aspect of school education has been comprehensively neglected for two reasons. The Puritan–Victorian tradition considered that experience of enjoyment was a waste of time, if not positively sinful; also, school examiners found that subjects that are aesthetic and practical are more difficult to assess. It is noticeable that education for enjoyment plays a progressively smaller part in formal education as the pupil grows older; this is mainly the result of following an examination-orientated syllabus. The main function of the secondary schools has been that of containment. The children's energy has been contained in a series of classrooms which enclose space, and a series of set subjects which enclose knowledge. More and more young people are becoming dissatisfied with an adolescence spent in preparing for an adult life. They want to lead a full life in the present, and their present life is, paradoxically, the best preparation for their future adult life.

The schools in future must arrange a more regular routine for young people to find enjoyment in pursuing their own inclinations. It is important that children should be provided with a sufficient variety of materials and experiences to give them a wide choice of activities for their leisure time. Increased attention must be attached to direct instruction in drama, film, the arts and crafts and sports as an essential part of everyday learning. Education for enjoyment must be taken seriously, and should also be extended to young people who have left school, and to adults. Playing fields, gymnasia, libraries, and workrooms must somehow be made available to the community at large in the evenings and week-ends, and schools must become social centres. Parents and teachers must take every opportunity to refresh their own vision, allowing time for mental refreshment, and actively seeking it. They should frequently examine themselves to see if they have organised their own lives, so that their own achievements are self-gratifying. In this Utopia, parents would not find it necessary to seek fulfilment in their children's performances, and teachers would be ideal exemplars of the value of the creative process.

Many factors in society inhibit creativity: the loss of in-dividuality in the pressures towards conformity, the prevailing atmosphere of tension and anxiety, the advancement of techno-logy and science (themselves the products of creativity), an over-concern with materialism, and a demand that education should primarily provide the way to enhanced social status and a materially safe way of life. Yet these forces of negation co-exist with a longer life expectation and more leisure time. The arts in particular insist that emotional, aesthetic and expressional experi-ences can make a genuine contribution towards emotional stability and a richer use of leisure because the sensitivity of individuals to the world around them is awakened. This sensi-tivity can be regarded as the first step in creativity. The world of the arts is essentially one that has been created by artists, poets, writers, dramatists and composers, who have perceived the world in ways different from their contemporaries.

A general upsurge of interest in creativity is certain to have a very beneficial effect. Most people in Britain and the U.S.A. have shown themselves indifferent to the arts. Perhaps this is a tradition inherited from the Puritans who found beauty in plainness; perhaps it is an attitude handed down from the time when most people (even successful capitalists) were too busy earning a living or making a fortune to have time to cultivate the arts; or perhaps the social tradition that regarded the enjoyment of the arts as effeminate led to their being ignored by the men and their male offspring. Whatever the reason, the arts, even more so than sport, have been treated as spectator pleasures, and active par-ticipation has been usually left to the highly creative. A general movement towards creativity could make thousands (even those who are relatively low in the creative scale) feel that they were not so much experts as collaborators with genius. A new generation of artists, writers, poets, actors, dramatists and musical composers could emerge from this movement, but a more important result would be the giving to ordinary people a significant and satisfying sense of self-fulfilment hitherto denied them.

Every creative performance involves an evaluation of the results. Creativity can never be dissociated from the creative product, which represents the solution of the creator's problem: for in every truly creative work there is no one correct answer or predetermined solution. The individual is compelled to arrive at his own synthesis and conclusion. Evaluation, for the most part, must be individual and subjective; teacher and critic have their right of judgment, but praise or blame must be actively accepted or rejected by the creator. There cannot be passive submission. Any programme of learning inside or outside the school that does not include active participation debars the individual from creative experience. Further, critical thinking should be applied after and not before the production, and final evaluation is best suspended until ideas have been fully considered and freely expressed.

The word 'education' is derived from the Latin verbs *educare* ('to bring up a child') and *educere* ('to lead out of')—a bringing out of what is within. If the educationist's purpose is to nurture the child's innate capacities to the full and to give to people not merely an useful occupation but a full and abundant life, then the creative process must in every possible way be actively stimulated.

For the creative element is what is uniquely human in man. It is the most profound part of man's personality, the source of wonder and delight, and a means of attaining inner peace and harmony. It is only by fostering and nurturing it that civilization can be sustained and revitalised.

References

DE BONO, E. *The Use of Lateral Thinking*. London: Cape, 1967.
MALTZMAN, L., SIMON, S., RASKIN, D., and LICHT, L. 'Experimental Studies on the Training of Originality'. *Psychological Monographs*, **LXXIV**, 1960 (493).
OSBORN, A. F. *Applied Imagination*. New York: Scribner, 1957.
PARKER, S. R. 'Retrospective "Bridging" of Three Occupational Groups'. *Sociology*, **I**, January 1967.
TORRANCE, E. P. *Guiding Creative Talent*. Englewood Cliffs, N.J.: Prentice-Hall, 1962.

Further Reading

BANKS, J. A. 'The Sociology of Work'. In FYVEL, T. R. (ed.) *The Frontiers of Society*. London: Cohen and West, 1964.

BRACKENBURG, A. 'Creative Education and the Musician'. *New Era*, **49,** June 1968.

BRAY, D. W. *Issues in the Study of Talent*. New York: King's Crown Press (Columbia University Press), 1954.

BLOOM, B. S. *Stability and Change in Human Characteristics*. New York: John Wiley, 1964.

BROOME, V. *The Problem of Progress*. London: Cassell, 1963.

DAVIES, B. D., and GIBSON, A. *The Social Education of the Adolescent*. London: University of London Press, 1967.

FRASER, R. (ed.) *Work*. Harmondsworth: Penguin Books, 1968.

GIDDENS, A. 'Notes on the Concepts of Play and Leisure'. *Sociological Review*, **12,** 1, 1964.

GINSBERG, M. *The Idea of Progress—A Revaluation*. London: Methuen, 1953.

HAGGARD, E. A. 'Socialisation, Personality and Academic Achievement in Gifted Children'. *School Review*, **65,** Winter 1957.

HAVINGHURST, R. J. *Human Development and Education*. New York: McKay, 1953.

KING, A. 'Revolution in Education'. *The Listener*, **LXXVI,** 1 September 1966.

LANTON, W. C. 'Educating Children for Tomorrow's World— An International Challenge'. *Education for Teaching*, **75,** Spring 1968.

LOWENFELD, V. *Creative and Mental Growth*. New York: Macmillan, 1957.

MCCLELLAND, D. C., *et al. Talent and Society*. New York: Van Nostrand, 1958.

MILGRAM, S. 'Nationality and Conformity'. *Scientific American*, **205,** 1961.

OMEN, J. W. 'Some Observations on Physical Education and Leisure'. *Physical Education*, **61,** March 1969.

PATTERSON, H. 'The Creative Image in Liberal Studies'. *Education Today*, **117,** 4, July 1967.

PETERSON, A. D. C. *The Future of Education*. London: Cresset Press (Barrie and Jenkins), 1968.

PETTER, G. S. V. 'Recreation and the Creative Arts'. *Trends in Education*, **15,** July 1969.

RUBENSTEIN, D., and STONEMAN, C. (eds.) *Education for Democracy*. Harmondsworth: Penguin Books, 1970.

THOMSON, G. *The Foreseeable Future*. London: Cambridge University Press, 2nd edition, 1960.

VAIZEY, J. *Education for Tomorrow*. Harmondsworth: Penguin Books, 1966.

WARREN, A. 'Creative Activities and Social Attitudes'. *Technical Journal*, **6,** 4, May 1968.

WHITEHEAD, N. J. 'A Pilot Investigation of the Leisure Activities of Young and Mature Adults in the City of York'. *Physical Education Research Paper No. 4*. Leeds: Carnegie College, July 1967.

WRAGG, M. 'The Leisure Activities of Boys and Girls'. *Educational Research*, **10,** February 1968.

YOUNG, M. *The Rise of the Meritocracy*. London: Thames and Hudson, 1961.

Index